Money
Secrets

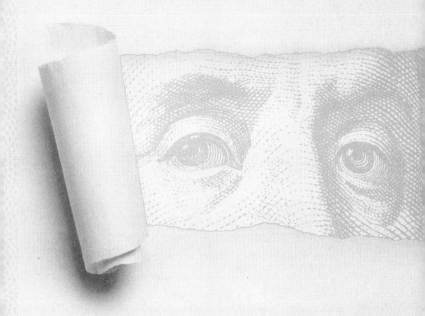

Keys to Smart Investing

Kim Curtis
CFP, ChFC, CLU, CAP, AEP, MSFS

MONEY SECRETS
Kim Curtis CFP®, ChFC®, CLU®, CAP®, AEP®, MSFS

Copies of this book may be purchased for educational, business, or promotional use.
Please contact Financial Literacy Press at 303-753-7578 or write to Financial Literacy Press,
care of the author at *KimCurtis@FinancialLiteracyPress.com*.

Cover design: Kathi Dunn, Dunn+Associates
Interior design: Rebecca Finkel, F+P Graphic Design
Publisher: Financial Literacy Press
Book Consultant: Judith Briles, The Book Shepherd
Editor: Shari Caudron

Library of Congress Catalog Number:
ISBN hardcover: 978-0-9913166-0-1
ISBN paperback: 978-0-9913166-3-2
ISBN ebook: 978-0-9913166-1-8
ISBN audio: 978-0-9913166-2-5

Library of Congress Cataloging-in-Publication Data on file
Categories for cataloging and shelving:
1. Business   2. Personal Finance   3. Investing   4. Wealth Management

10 9 8 7 6 5 4 3 2 1

Printed in Canada

To my family, with gratitude.

CONTENTS

PROLOGUE

A moment's insight is sometimes

worth a life's experience.

—OLIVER WENDELL HOLMES

Let's start with the obvious: money makes people anxious. It doesn't matter how old you are or how much money you make. Money questions plague all of us at one time or another and penetrate every aspect of our lives. Do I have enough? Will I have enough? What is enough?

I hear these questions every day in my work as a financial advisor—from parents; newly middle-aged couples questioning how they can support their college-age kids and their elderly parents; from newly divorced women afraid they can't make it on their own; and from retired couples fearful their nest egg is insufficient.

Added to all this very real anxiety is the shame many people feel around money. They're ashamed because they don't know how to manage their money, because they've been ignoring their financial life for years, and because money—or the lack thereof—makes them feel inadequate.

I've been there. I know what fear, shame, loneliness and inadequacy feel like.

• • •

I grew up in a small, rural farming community in upstate New York, the kind of place where everybody knew everyone. One day when I was fourteen, my parents told my two sisters and me they were getting divorced and my mother would gain full custody. Because my mom had dropped out of school to marry, and because she'd never worked, her job prospects were limited. Desperate, she took a job at our high school cafeteria. It was the only job that allowed her to have the same schedule as her daughters.

Unfortunately, the money she made wasn't nearly enough to support us, so she applied for—and received—government-assisted school lunches. To get the free lunch, I had to hand a red paper ticket to the cashier. I was deeply ashamed of that red ticket and all it meant—that my dad was gone. That my mom couldn't afford lunches and that we were poor.

I did everything I could to make sure no one would see the cashier putting the red ticket into the till. I'd find the line farthest from my friends. I'd wait until a line was empty. I'd hide the ticket underneath my plate.

That red ticket was a measurement, a standard of comparison. It set me apart at school, made me feel less deserving, and was the beginning of my anxiety around the scarcity of money.

Fortunately, the value of education was ingrained in my psyche. I had watched my mother work hard to obtain her General Education Development (GED) certification, put herself through community college and study to become a successful Realtor®.

Following her example, I put myself through college and then law school. While job hunting, I worked in a luggage store owned by my roommate's family. Since I was under-employed and had never learned to manage money (because we never had any), I defaulted on my school loans, condemning myself to a long period of financial debt and bad credit. The debt strangled my sense of self, immersing me in guilt, doubt and feelings of incompetency. I had obtained a good education. But money?

Money was something other people had—but not me.

What I did have, however, was a friend who believed in me and helped me get on track financially by anonymously making a payment on my student loan. One day, when the bill arrived I noticed my balance had gone down, not up. Confused, I asked family and friends if they knew anyone who had made a payment on my behalf, and the generosity of my dear friend, Joyce Briggs, was revealed.

Her gift made me stop and realize the untrue story I had been telling myself—that money was scarce and I didn't deserve it. Thanks to her gift, I became conscious of my internal money talk and began to take my desire for money and the anxiety that surrounded it more seriously. Slowly, I began to believe in my ability to earn and manage money and, in the process, the fear, anxiety, inaction, blame and guilt I had around money slowly evaporated. I will be forever grateful to Joyce, whom I now consider my guardian angel. Her belief in my abilities provided an awakening that transformed my relationship with money.

It would be a decade before I started working in the financial services industry, but my early experiences with money taught me something I share with clients: you don't need a master's degree in finance or an alphabet of professional designations after your name to understand how to have a satisfying, worry-free relationship with your money. You simply need the *willingness* and *courage* to confront your fears, desires, and fantasies around money.

This book is your gift. For whatever reason it landed in your hands, trust it, allow for the journey to unfold. Be open, willing, and courageous … it is time.

CHAPTER 1

IT'S TIME TO TAKE CHARGE

Change is avalanching upon our heads and most

people are grotesquely unprepared to cope with it.

—ALVIN TOFFLER, *Future Shock*

Chances are you've had some moment during which you decided to become smarter about your money. That money moment might have come in the wake of a divorce, on the brink of retirement, or after spending money on an extravagant purchase that made sense at the time, but in retrospect, was financially foolish.

Money moments nearly always cause anxiety—*Is my money safe? Why did I buy that? Will I have to work forever? Am I financially secure?*—and they happen to each and every one of us at some point. These money-conscious moments are ultimately beneficial because they force us to pause—and present an opportunity to take charge of our finances.

But when money moments happen, they cause pain. And right now, there are more people suffering more painful money moments than at any time in history. Why? Because all of us are being called upon to manage our money in ways we never had to before.

The Decline of Retirement Security

It used to be that company pensions, personal savings and Social Security—the three-legged income stool—supported us during retirement. If you were born before 1960, when this support system was relatively solid and dependable, you started working and acquiring assets with the belief you could retire and be relatively worry-free about the financial costs of housing, food and health care.

But over the last four decades, each leg of the stool has fractured.

To begin with, company pension plans (called defined-benefit plans) are largely a thing of the past. In the 1970s, 60 percent of companies offered pension plans. Under this arrangement, workers typically committed their careers to one employer and the employer returned the favor by funding their employees' retirements. My father, for instance, worked for Ford Motor

Company all his working life and he retired with a comfortable pension, receiving a fixed dollar amount into his checking account each month.

But today, less than seven percent of companies offer pension plans. As a result, the burden of saving for retirement has shifted from the company to the worker in the form of defined-contribution plans, such as 401(k) or 403(b) plans.

Retirement Plan Trends

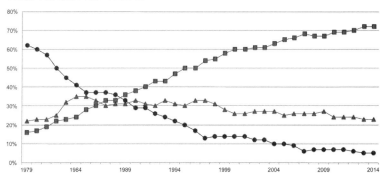

"Private-Sector Workers Participating in an Employment-Based Retirement Plan," Employee Benefit Research Institute. http://www.ebri.org/publications/benfaq/index.cfm?fa=retfaqt14fig2
*2014 is based on projections, not actual study.

—●— Defined Benefit
—■— Defined Contribution Only
—▲— Both

The decline of pension plans means most Americans are having to make up the shortfall with their own savings. The problem is that the average American is woefully undisciplined when it comes to saving money, saving less than five percent of their annual income per year.

Typically, saving less than five percent of your gross income per year would make it very difficult to have enough money to fund retirement. The fact that life expectancy in America increased from an average of 65 to 79 years of age in a single generation (and continues to climb), means most of us have to plan for many more years without any earned income.

Average Household Savings Rate

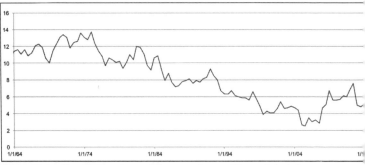

Personal Savings Rate, US Department of Commerce: Bureau of Economic Analysis,
http://research.stlouisfed.org/fred2/series/PSAVERT/

Even in retirement, today's retirees look and act nothing like retirees a generation ago. Today's retirees are thinking, and doing, the "next" in their lives. The biggest group of entrepreneurs today is the post-55 crowd, a crowd that is starting new businesses beyond anyone's original imagination. With retirees more active, they have a greater need for more money and thus more savings or they are continuing to work to support themselves.

The third big change in the retirement picture is that Social Security, the government-managed social-support system most of us have contributed to with every paycheck, is no longer reliable. Social Security was created when life spans were shorter and the government didn't need to support people for decades after they stopped working. Now that people are living longer and the population as a whole is aging, the government is paying out far more money than it takes in. This means the current system is unsustainable. Changes to Social Security, such as delaying the age at which benefits are received or adjusting down the annual cost-of-living increases, will need to be made.

> Social Security as we know it today probably will not be the Social Security of tomorrow.

So this is where we are now: company pensions have disappeared, personal savings are insufficient, and Social Security is on shaky ground. This perfect storm of events means you need to pay serious attention to how you envision and fund your retirement.

But … *how*?

The Big Lie

Wall Street, the center of America's financial world, seduces Americans with the promise of easy investment riches. Buy low! Sell high! Greed is good! Go for it!

The media communicates a different and more confusing message: Be afraid! Unemployment is rising! Healthcare costs are escalating! Your money isn't safe! After stirring your anxiety, does the media then tell you how to quell your fears through smart investing and saving? No. The media encourages you to buy more stuff to make yourself feel better—handbags, shoes, watches, age-defying cosmetics, cars, second homes.

Then your "friends," the investment brokers, come forward and promise to help with your investments. But what you must understand is that brokers are in the business of *sales*, and they will advise you to buy what they are selling—not necessarily what is best for your individual portfolio.

Do you feel a churning in the pit of your stomach? I feel it, and I've got the know-how to avoid these traps. That fear is exactly what the financial services industry—investment magazines, mutual fund firms and stockbrokers—want you to feel. They want you afraid. They want you confused. They want to keep you ignorant so that you'll pay for answers ... or relief. That is how the industry makes money.

The fear the industry generates makes me angry. It should make you angry as well.

Mystified, overwhelmed and anxious, many Americans are choosing to do nothing when it comes to investing, which only increases the insecurity they already have about money.

It doesn't have to be this way. No one has to live with financial anxiety and paralysis. You can learn the basic elements of investing and how to work with a qualified, independent and objective financial advisor. The financial services industry works hard to keep its money secrets to itself. This book will reveal those secrets to you.

I wrote *Money Secrets* to demystify investing and show you how to take charge of your finances and your future. Although investing is not simple, it is not as complicated as Wall Street wants you to believe.

Money Secrets starts with a simple premise: if the person you've chosen to manage your investments is in the business of sales, you probably should get rid of him or her. Very few financial advisors—less than 10 percent—are legally obliged to have your best interests in mind. This book will help you learn how to pick a qualified and legally responsible advisor; develop a personalized, integrated financial plan; and understand different investment options. The book also translates the basic components of smart investing into a language you can understand.

Money Secrets isn't a book about how to create a financial plan, although it does cover why an integrated financial plan is necessary. Nor is this a book about how to become a do-it-yourself investor. Too many Americans have already tried that with little financial success. Instead, this book will teach you how to collaborate with a qualified advisor to create the financial future necessary to achieve your life's dreams.

Whatever money moment brought you to this book—fear, loss, anxiety, determination, desire, hope—be assured this book will give you the foundation you need to make smart, confident and empowered decisions about your money.

Are you ready?

Let's get started!

CHAPTER 2

ADOPTING THE RIGHT MINDSET

If your mind can conceive it, you can achieve it.

—NAPOLEON HILL, *Think and Grow Rich*

I have no special talents,
I am only passionately curious.

—ALBERT EINSTEIN

At the most basic level, money is a symbol of value. But money can also be an intensely personal and emotional subject. What we are willing to pay for something typically reflects deeply held values. To better understand how emotional money can be, I invite you to pause and think about your relationship with money.

- Do discussions *about* money make you anxious?
- Do you constantly *put off* financial decisions?
- Do you *abdicate* big money decisions to your spouse?

- Does the whole financial and investing world seem *too big* and *confusing* and *jammed* with jargon for you to understand?

- Would you rather do almost *anything* than create a financial plan?

If your answer to any of these questions is "yes," you're in good company. Nearly every individual or couple I've worked with has, at some point, been anxious about money and their ability to create a secure financial future for themselves. In fact, not a day goes by when I don't hear some variation of one of these lines:

I've been accumulating a lot of stuff—a house, a 401(k) plan, some stocks—but I have no real financial plan.

Thinking about financial planning is scary;
when I went to call you I started to cry.
I know ignorance is driving this emotion.

I need a sense of control over my money but don't know how to get it.

Maybe if I marry, my financial future
will be more secure.

I dodged the layoff bullet probably five times but now it really does look like my days are numbered. I'm worried about healthcare costs and I have no pension.

I am naturally a skeptic, show me your data
and prove to me your process and success.

When I was married, I asked my husband
if I could sit in on meetings with the advisor
and accountant. He said I would be bored
so I never pressed the issue. Now that
I'm divorced, I am learning for the first
time how to invest and how
clueless I had been about money.

I bought all these gold coins in a panic
when the stock market was down.
Now they are worth a lot less than
what I paid for them.

My wife expects me to handle the investments,
but in truth, I am uncomfortable with
the burden—and not very good at it.

I feel poor all the time, even though
I make good money. I have no focus or
priorities based on what's important
to me, so I spend, spend, spend.

I'm frugal with a lot of things,
but then I'll go to Target or Costco
and spend $300 without blinking.

I do not trust myself. I sold out at the bottom
and now must work to recover.

My father told me I needed $3,000,000
to retire comfortably. That has always been
my benchmark without knowing why,
or if, it really applies to me.

My parents lived paycheck to paycheck.
I do not want to repeat their legacy.

I want a plan that will make me
feel empowered and give me a
sense of control.

Do any of these comments sound familiar?

In every one of these cases—let me repeat: in every one—the more conscious the client became about money, the more capable and confident he or she became about his or her financial future.

The point I'm trying to make is that once you decide to become more mindful of your financial choices, you move from anxiety *(Money scares me),* to relief *(I'm finally doing something about this!),* to excitement *(Wow! This isn't as hard as I thought),* to certainty *(I can and will create the stress-free financial future I desire).* Ultimately, by the time you create an integrated financial plan, you will feel utterly in control of your destiny—not just with money, but in life.

I can promise this because I've worked with countless individuals and couples who originally had little sense of their monthly spending or overall net worth. But as we worked together to create a financial plan, they acquired the ability to make wise financial choices. "Now, money is no longer leading me," they frequently tell me. "I'm leading it."

You, too, can gain feelings of confidence and mastery around money. But the process doesn't start with external investing, as many advisors would have you believe. It starts with the desire to understand your own internal relationship to money.

Your Personal Money Story

At Wealth Legacy Institute, I created a process we call Humanigraphix™. Think of Humanigraphix as a pictorial mapping of your family tree. It's a practical framework for understanding your family history, the subconscious family patterns and beliefs you may have acquired about money, and the life events that may affect your planning.

Just as spoken language organizes your thought processes, the Humanigraphix process helps you think about how important events and relationships are related to patterns of wealth and money. The process helps you see the larger picture, to view financial issues in their current and historical context.

Below is an example of a Humanigraphix chart. I encourage you to use the model to create your own. How? By plotting your family history and looking for patterns around money, relation-ships and values. You might also consider your family history as it relates to gender, as well as socioeconomic, cultural, religious and political influences. (*The Appendix includes questions to get you started.*)

Humanigraphix™

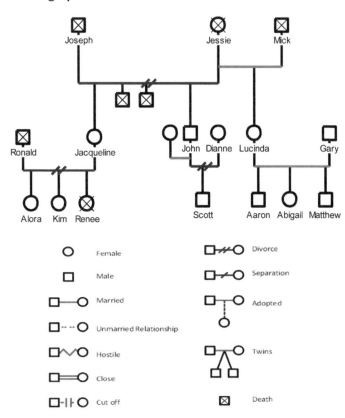

One of the most exciting aspects of Humanigraphix is the way it leads individuals and families beyond the one-dimensional linear perspectives that typically characterize financial planning. ("I want to have this much money by this deadline.") Instead, Humanigraphix helps you think systemically about money, because as soon as you notice one pattern or belief related to money (i.e., that private education is too expensive) your vision expands allowing you to notice other patterns as well. In my own Humanigraphix chart, what stood out was the number of divorces across generations. Going deeper, I realized the women in my family history were all married before age 18. These observations helped me better understand my mother, my grandmother and my great grandmother with regards to resiliency and economic independence. It definitely explains why my mother had education as such a high family value.

> The more *conscious* you become about money, the more capable and confident you become about your financial future.

What is Your Motivation Toward Money?

Traditional financial planning typically focuses on external objectives, e.g., creating retirement income strategies and estate transfer plans, identifying cash flow and debt management, reducing risk in an undiversified portfolio, managing 401(k) distributions and/or minimizing your tax liability.

All of these are necessary and important steps toward financial security, but the first—and I would argue—most important step is understanding your emotional orientation to money.

Generally speaking, people regard money in three ways. They focus on the:

- *past* (experiences they have already had around money)
- *present* (achieving and securing current money needs)
- *future* (focusing on dreams and possibilities)

All of us are, at one point or another, past, present and future thinkers when it comes to money. But, typically, each of us has a primary motivation that guides our thinking.

Think of the last time you decided to embark on a new fitness regimen. Thinking about this new plan (future) you became committed. You stocked up on healthy foods, purchased your new crossfit training shoes and got ready to start the program (present). You may have even followed the program for two or five or seven days. But then one day you got distracted and stopped. The old you showed up with all your past habits and routines. What sounded good a few days ago was suddenly pushed aside.

Money works the same way. Whether investing, saving, spending, or sharing, what may have started out as a strong, clearly motivated financial strategy suddenly gets usurped by another equally compelling motivation. How you think about money, whether you are past, present or future dominant, ultimately determines whether you succeed or stay stuck.

Let's look at each of these orientations in more detail.

PAST THINKERS: If you are past-focused, you may not believe there is a problem regarding money. You may simply not know what you do not know. You may be spending down your retirement savings, for example, financially enabling your adult children, or living with some form of financial chaos, e.g., blaming others for your current financial situation.

You may also let anxiety about money issues from the past (your story, beliefs, assumptions, or judgments) guide you today, in particular, by focusing on problems in the external world. You may worry about paying too much in taxes, for example, be overly concerned with the volatility of the stock market, and/or worry whenever the inflation rate rises. In short, past thinkers are anxious. They crave order, don't readily accept change, and can be too cautious. On the plus side, past thinkers tend to be pragmatic. They may worry about taxes, but they also have their charitable contributions in place.

PRESENT THINKERS: If you are present-focused, you are a doer who is conscious of the current state of your day-to-day finances. If you are not happy with your current situation, you are willing to acknowledge that you may be responsible for the current state of affairs. You probably understand your monthly cash flow, have adequate insurance, read financial statements, and may even know your net worth. You are also open to gathering more information to learn about possible solutions.

But present thinkers can sometimes be too practical. They may be so focused on the daily tasks that they ignore their financial future altogether. While present thinkers are not obsessed by problems and/or past mistakes, they also are not paying attention to the grander, future vision of their life.

FUTURE THINKERS: If you are a future thinker, you are focused on setting goals, making changes, and continually improving your financial vision for the future. You are full of dreams and possibilities, and are aspiring to develop and grow. If this describes you, congratulations! Now would be a good time to create an action plan for carrying out the desired changes.

But as important as it is to consider the future, future thinkers may have a tendency to rely too much on intuition. Instead of basing their financial decisions on empirical data, they may lead with their gut. They might also have a tendency to ignore their current financial picture, or overlook legitimate external concerns like taxes. And, they are sometimes procrastinators—they have big vision, but need help in implementation.

Which motivation are you? Are you predominately a *past, present or future thinker?* What stage do you find yourself in most often?

All investors need the capacity to evaluate the past, understand the present and plan for the future. But you don't want to get stuck in habitual thinking. By understanding your *primary* motivation toward money, you can begin to develop the strengths and perspective to move beyond your present circumstances into the possibilities of your ideal future.

> How you deal with money is how you deal with life.

Launching Your Financial Transformation

You may have guessed when reading about the three motivations, that there is a lot of overlap between how you think about money and how you think about other issues in your life. Some people are naturally more focused on risks and problems (past thinkers); others are always anticipating what's next (future thinkers).

Given the power of money to both influence your actions and reveal your inner thoughts and beliefs, it makes sense to start your financial education by understanding what you want and need to be happy—not just financially but in life.

Questions to Ask Yourself

1. What is the best and highest vision for yourself and your family?

   Get comfortable and fully imagine your highest vision.

   Where are you living?

   What kind of work are you doing?

   How are you contributing to others?

   What are your relationships with friends, family and community like?

   What gives your life meaning and a sense of purpose?

   What makes you feel good about yourself?

2. As you think about these things, be as specific as you can.

   What does your house look like?

   What are you doing for fun … and how often?

   How much money do you have in the bank?

   How much is that money growing each year?

3. After you have this vision in mind, *write it down* as if it is already happening. Start your written vision with the words, "*I am …*"

   Don't make the vision sound like something you "hope" to achieve; make it sound as if you are doing all of these things right now. "I am planning my family's annual trip to Europe from the deck of my mountain home …."

4. Then—and this is the important part—revisit that vision every day.

   See the vision. Feel the vision. Feel the energy and excitement that are created when you believe, truly believe, this is your future.

Reading your vision regularly will help you become convinced that what your imagination has created *is* your future reality. After all, everything you do in life is merely an external manifestation of what has already occurred in your mind.

Once you have identified this highest vision for yourself, keep reading this book and get the money secrets to gain the financial competency and peace of mind you've been craving for years.

> *Being clueless about money*
> *is no longer affordable.*
> —KATE LEVINSON, PHD

CHAPTER 3

WHO CAN YOU TRUST?

The investor's chief problem—and even his

worst enemy—is likely to be himself.

—BENJAMIN GRAHAM,
commonly known as the father of Value Investing

Wisdom is pure intelligence before the

contamination of thought.

—SYDNEY BANKS,
author and philosopher

In recent years, the news has been loaded with stories about innocent and sophisticated investors who've lost their life savings by trusting the wrong advisor. Securities fraud, accounting scandals, corporate misconduct, and Ponzi schemes are a few of the ways trusting investors have been conned.

My heart grieves when I think of all the innocent people who have unknowingly trusted an advisor, which is why I wrote this book. Every profession attracts predators. Mine is no different.

Because of this, I wouldn't blame you if you decided to take charge of your own investing. With the proliferation of financial news sources, it would seem relatively easy to manage a portfolio. Read a few articles, do a few calculations, and *voila*! Your money is invested and safe because you're in charge … *right*?

Wrong.

Very wrong.

If you are trying to manage your own investments, you are making one of the most costly mistakes any investor can make. Why? Because financial markets are complex and the odds are stacked against you.

According to DALBAR®, an independent third-party research firm, people who take responsibility for their stock and bond investments generate returns that are on average 50 percent *lower* than the typical market index. This means that over twenty years the average investor with a $100,000 portfolio would have earned just $129,890. By comparison, the S&P 500 earned $384,560—a difference of $254,670!

Because of the enormous potential for loss, the first advisor you want to fire in your take-no-prisoners investment strategy is most likely yourself.

Average Investor vs. Markets
January 1, 1992 to December 31, 2013

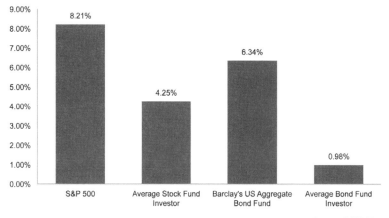

Source: DALBAR

The **Average Investor vs. Markets** graph illustrates annualized average investor returns compared to the markets over a 20-year period. As you can see, the S&P 500 (a fund comprised of all the stocks in the Standard & Poor's 500) would have generated an average annual rate of return of 8.21 percent. However, the average stock fund investor would have generated an average return of just 4.25 percent. In the bond market, individual investors fared even worse. The aggregate bond fund (a representative collection of all bonds) generated an average annual return of 6.34 percent; the individual bond fund investor, however, generated a return of less than 1 percent.

Markets Don't Fail, Investors Do

There are many reasons individual investors don't fare as well as markets and they all boil down to this: investors are human and humans are inherently emotional. When markets are up, we're greedy and overconfident. When markets are down, we're scared.

The continual up-down, confidence-fear cycle means that statistically speaking, people almost always buy and sell stock at the wrong time. We buy at market peaks when surrounded by good news and we sell at market lows when fear kicks in.

Think back on the behavior of someone you know during the Great Recession. For most, it was not a pretty picture; 69 percent of US investors sold at or near the bottom which occurred on March 9, 2009. Can you believe that? Think about what that means ... whatever the portfolio value was, by panic selling, their investment value dropped to almost half.

> Avoiding potential loss also prevents potential gain.

To build wealth over the long term, you have to fight against the human drive to maximize pleasure and minimize pain. In fact, you have to do just the opposite. As the legendary mutual fund pioneer Sir John Templeton said, "The time of maximum pessimism is the best time to buy and the time of maximum optimism is the best time to sell."

Behavioral Biases

Greed and fear are not the only behaviors that work against individual investors. Some of the other reasons you should not take charge of your own investments include:

Narrow Focus: Many investors tend to consider investment decisions in isolation without looking at their entire portfolio. They'll purchase a particular stock or stock fund without considering the tax consequences, the overall mix of high- and low-risk in their portfolio, and how the stock fits into both short- and long-term time horizons. Some investments that look risky on their own might actually be a valuable addition to the overall portfolio.

Short-Term Decision Making: Investors typically base stock or stock fund purchase decisions on anticipated performance over short time frames, i.e., several months or less. But the potential for loss is much greater during this time period. Historically speaking, in any given month the average stock will fall in value about 40 percent of the time. However, the probability of a loss drops to 25 percent over a year, 19 percent over five years, 7 percent over ten years, and almost never over twenty years. Simply put, if you want to build wealth—and avoid losses, you must acquire the discipline to buy and hold investments for a long time.

Loss Aversion: Investors feel the pain of loss twice as deeply as they do pleasure from an equivalent gain. In an attempt to avoid these painful losses, many investors choose to sit on uninvested cash rather than invest it at the wrong time. How many of you are still in cash with no plan on how to get back on track? Unfortunately, avoiding potential loss also prevents potential gain.

Over-Confidence: If you've been successful in other areas of life, it would be easy to assume you could also be successful at investing. But financial markets can be complicated, and success in life does not necessarily translate to success in investing.

Action Bias: All of us like to feel in control of our lives. In investing, that need for control often shows up in the form of buying and selling too frequently. If markets are volatile, many will trade simply to feel like they are doing *something.* But the more you trade, the higher your costs, and the more likely the trade will be based on emotion rather than a solid long-term investment strategy.

Most of us do not want to think we have a bias. We don't want to think we are action adverse, or myopic in our decision-making ability. But the more clearly you can see your biases, the more skilled you'll become in making financial decisions that are right for you and your family.

Hiring an Advisor

The most valuable step you can take is to find a competent, trustworthy advisor to help manage your financial life. Once you have found the right advisor, the rewards of having an advocate and steward for you and your family can be profound and life changing.

Who is your current source for investment advice? Is it an uncle, co-worker, neighbor, broker, magazine or online columnist? All too often advisors are selected based on referrals from people we know, an affiliation at church, for example, or a good friend. Many times that affiliation or good friend does not have your unique profile. What has worked for them, in other words, may not work for you.

Unfortunately, these referrals are often not the best way to find a qualified advisor. With your financial future at stake, you want to select a competent financial advisor the same way you would a medical practitioner. Just as you wouldn't expect a pediatrician to manage heart surgery, you shouldn't ask someone in the business of selling investment products to create a financial plan for you.

There are no two ways about it: if you are serious about achieving your financial goals and do not have the time, desire, discipline, or expertise to actively plan and manage your financial life, you should seek help from a qualified professional advisor. There are a variety of professionals who work in the financial industry. Knowing who they are and what they can do for you is important.

So … where can you find an advisor who has your best interests at heart?

Brokers and securities salespeople will tell you they are on your side and have your best interests in mind. But as Paul Merriman says in his book, *Get Smart or Get Screwed*, being on your side is nice emotionally, but it's much more important and valuable for someone to be on your side legally where it counts.

Whether your advisor is on your side legally is the biggest dividing line between who you should hire and who you should fire! Unfortunately it is hard to determine who has legal responsibility to act in your best interests.

Start by learning THE best-kept money secret of all: *Ninety-one percent of so-called financial advisors are in the business of sales.* They are brokers or "registered representatives" who work for or are affiliated with brokerage firms, banks, mutual funds, and insurance companies. They make their money by selling you products from their employer's grab bags. Many of the commissions are built into the cost so you can't see the actual price you pay.

Where do you find these sales-agents-masquerading-as-advisors? Everywhere. Wall Street brokers trained to sell you the sizzle, not the steak. They want you excited and in a buying mood. But investments should be boring—if you are buying when excited, you may be buying out of emotion (or because of your advisor's talent for sales), not logic.

91% of Advisors in Sales

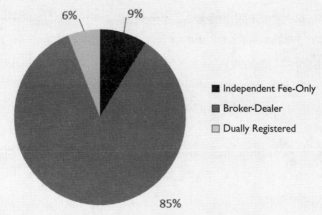

6% 9%

■ Independent Fee-Only
■ Broker-Dealer
☐ Dually Registered

85%

Registered Investment Advisor (RIA) – Fiduciary

Fiduciaries must put your interests ahead of their own and must disclose any real or potential conflicts of interest, including compensation and referrals from companies that sell investments. A fiduciary must not only avoid financial harm but also do what is in your best financial interest.

Broker-Dealer – Suitability

A securities broker-dealer is a salesperson (registered representative) who works for a securities brokerage firm, such as a bank, insurance company, wire house, or independent brokerage. He recommends products that are suitable for you that do not harm you.

Dually Registered – Both

An individual or firm that plays both sides of the coin, acting both as a salesperson and financial fiduciary, based on convenience.

Even financial advisors who call themselves independent advisors are often affiliated with broker-dealers, such as LPL Financial, Raymond James, Ameriprise, Lincoln Financial, Commonwealth, and AXA. This group of advisors consists of financial fiduciaries that are also making commissions on certain products and investments, making it difficult for investors to know when their advisor is getting a commission or a kickback for the product he or she recommends.

> Only one out of ten financial advisors is serving as your financial fiduciary 100 percent of the time.

To get past all the smoke and mirrors and learn if your advisor is representing you—or his or her company, simply ask if he or she is a *registered representative* and/or holds a Series 6 or 7 license. A "yes" answer to either question means he or she is in the business of sales.

The Difference Between Fiduciary and Suitability

There are two levels of legal accountability—fiduciary or suitability—and knowing the distinction between the two will be extremely important to your financial success and pocketbook.

Instead of risking your nest egg with someone who has simply slapped the term financial advisor on his or her business card, what you need is a financial *fiduciary*, a trusted advisor who has legal obligation to act at all times with your best interest in mind. (Lawyers and accountants are also fiduciary.) *Basically,*

ONLY one out of ten financial advisors is serving as your financial fiduciary 100 percent of the time.

The Securities Exchange Commission (SEC) identifies five responsibilities of fiduciaries. They:
1. put clients' interests first;
2. act with the utmost good faith;
3. provide full and fair disclosure of all material facts;
4. don't mislead clients; and
5. expose all conflicts of interest to clients.

Think about choosing a surgeon. Which standard of care would you want for your operation? A doctor who was required to worry only about not harming you or a doctor who was required to provide the best care for your individual health situation? Identifying the best course of action for *your* particular situation is what defines a fiduciary.

Let's look at *suitability* accountability. What's the difference between suitability and fiduciary accountability? Let's say you hire your brother-in-law to find and purchase a vehicle for you. You have $40,000 to spend and you want to buy a hybrid vehicle. The list of "suitable" vehicles would give him ample discretion. If the "suitability" standard of care applied to your brother-in-law, he could pick any car that met your price and was a hybrid. He would not be under any obligation to explain to you (or anybody else) why he chose this vehicle as the best one for your particular situation.

Now … imagine if your brother-in-law received a kickback or commission from the car manufacturer for buying *your* car, but you then learned that other hybrid manufacturers did not offer him a commission on their cars. Would you rely on him to act solely in your best interest when he chooses your next vehicle?

Under the suitability rule, you could end up with a vehicle that is mustard yellow, has little storage and cramped seating, and was on sale in your price range because the dealer was having a hard time selling it. Legally, under the suitability rule, those issues wouldn't matter since the vehicle met your stated requirements of price and fuel efficiency.

Investment products may be less familiar than cars, yet your investments are far more important for your future than the type of car you drive. Because of this, you should accept no less than a fee-only financial fiduciary for your life and your future.

How Do Advisors Get Paid?

How your advisor gets paid often dictates how your money will be invested. Simply put: if you are the only one who writes a check, then you are in charge.

Advisors who accept commissions for selling you products have a conflict of interest. Advisors who receive wage income from their brokerage firm have a conflict of interest. Employees at banks and bank trust companies have a conflict of interest in two ways: by selling you the bank's mutual funds and then cross-selling you bank services.

Solid, objective financial advice is a valuable commodity and you should expect to pay a fair price for it. The founder of Vanguard, John Bogle, said, "While good advice may not be cheap, bad advice always costs you dearly, no matter how little you pay for it."

There are three basic ways an advisor gets paid:

Fee-only: Fee-only advisors charge fees one of three ways: by charging a percentage of assets managed, either through a flat fee, or an hourly rate. A percentage fee works this way: if your portfolio is worth $1 million, and your advisor charges 1 percent a year to manage the portfolio, you pay $10,000 a year or 0.25 percent quarterly which translates into $2,500 a quarter out of your investment portfolio for that service. This arrangement is often the best for a fiduciary relationship. Your advisor sells nothing; therefore they will look for low cost, efficient investments that keep as much money as possible in your pocket.

An advisor who does comprehensive financial planning will typically charge a planning fee that is separate from investment management advice. This fee is usually a flat fee depending on the complexity of your financial planning issues. A variation on this is charging hourly based on the time spent preparing the financial plan.

If an advisor tells you he provides financial planning services and his fee is built into his one percent charge for managing your investment assets, be wary. More often than not, under this arrangement your "financial plan" will be an investment plan.

An investment plan, on its own, is not likely to achieve your long-term retirement and legacy goals because an investment plan's focus is often not expansive enough. It typically does not take into account other elements such as life goals, estate planning, insurance, cash flow and tax issues.

Commissions: The financial services industry began with a commission model. A salesperson, e.g., a broker or advisor, convinces the buyer to make a purchase of a financial product, annuity, life insurance or mutual fund, and then a commission results from the sale. Obviously, under this arrangement, the broker may prefer you buy something that pays a larger commission. To the investor, it looks like someone else is paying the commission, but of course, the commission is paid by you, the investor.

Fee-based: Note the differences between fee-only arrangement, which is described above and is the preferred compensation arrangement, and fee-based compensation. Fee-based occurs when the broker gets paid both investment fees and commissions. This advisor works both sides of the compensation fence. He acts like he is on the same side as you are, yet he also receives incentives and commissions from products sold.

How Do You Find a Fee-Only Financial Fiduciary?

First, go to the National Association of Personal Financial Advisors (**NAPFA.org**) which is the country's leading professional association of fee-only financial advisors.

Second, ask a potential advisor if he or she is a fiduciary. Then, ask that person to sign a pledge that he or she will act as your fiduciary at all times and with all transactions. A broker (read: someone in the business of sales) would be extremely slow to sign such a pledge, knowing that falsely signing such a statement might get them in trouble later. If your advisor is not willing to sign the pledge, you have your answer. A fiduciary would not hesitate. *See the sample fiduciary oath in the Appendix.*

Third, ask the fiduciary if he or she also does financial planning. Creating a financial plan is an essential first step to building an investment portfolio that will meet your overall financial goals. Building an investment portfolio without first creating a financial plan is like mindlessly building a house without blueprints. You have to know your objectives before you can develop your plan.

Fourth, check the advisor's professional credentials. The initials "CFP®"—for CERTIFIED FINANCIAL PLANNER®—indicate that the advisor has successfully achieved the industry's gold standard by successfully completing the Certified Financial Planner Board of Standards initial and ongoing certification requirements.

Although bank trust departments follow a fiduciary standard, the bank fiduciary standard is less rigorous than the certified financial planner standard because bank trust companies can accept "revenue sharing" from investment products and they can utilize proprietary funds. This creates a conflict of interest between the trust company and you, the client.

Most brokers, whether employed by a bank, an independent brokerage firm, or a national brokerage firm, know when they have a conflict of interest with investors. Many dislike it. They have competent and intelligent people who want to help and do their best work. Unfortunately, without the *legal responsibility* of a fee-only financial fiduciary, it becomes difficult to give the very best advice, and you the client suffers.

The Seven C's for Picking an Advisor

Here are some other tips for choosing a qualified advisor:

Competence: Ask the advisor what experience and training he or she has had working with clients like you, i.e., recently divorced women, pre-retired couples, professionals, new widows, business owners. Also, knowing an advisor's formal educational background—both what he studied and where he went to school—may provide insight into his general intelligence, knowledge, and problem-solving ability.

Responding to direct-mail solicitation, accepting free meals with a seminar, or clicking on an Internet advertisement will NOT get you an ideal advisor.

Credentials: There are many credentials advisors can achieve, and these credentials provide further insight into the advisor's specialties and commitment to ongoing education. Some of these include CFP®, CFA® for Chartered Financial Analyst, ChFC® for Chartered Financial Consultant, and CLU® for

Chartered Life Underwriter. *See the Appendix for an abbreviated list of financial certifications and what they mean.*

Clean Record: See if complaints have been filed against the financial advisor you are considering. For unbiased information about advisors, go to **AdvisorInfo.SEC.gov**; for information on the advisor's business, go to **BBB.org**; for sales representatives and brokers, go to **BrokerCheck.FINRA.org**; for CFP® practitioners, go to **CFP.net**.

Client Service: Ask the advisor about the process for providing updates on the status of your accounts, as well as how often he will meet with you to revise and update your financial plan. At minimum, your advisor should meet with you once or twice a year to do four things:

1. Set annual goals;
2. Rebalance your portfolio;
3. Check the progress of your financial plan;
4. Create a year-end tax strategy.

Also, be sure to ask the advisor if he will be available to answer any just-in-time questions, such as leasing vs. buying a car or refinancing a mortgage.

Communication: Ideally, an advisor will assess your communication preferences to determine how best to work together. Do you prefer specifics and detail or bullet points and the big picture? Would you rather have formal, structured meetings or more relaxed, informal conversations? Also, how will communication occur—in person, over the phone, via e-mail? An advisor who understands your communication preferences will be able to communicate in a way that reinforces your long-term success.

Commitment to professional standards: A financial advisor must have a commitment to ethical behavior and high professional standards. This is often displayed by membership or affiliation to one or more professional organizations, such as the National Association of Personal Financial Advisors (NAPFA), Financial Planning Association (FPA), or National Association of Estate Planners and Councils (NAEPC).

Chemistry: Search for a financial advisor who listens to your concerns and answers questions in a way you understand. In addition to understanding your financial data, a competent advisor will want to know your emotions around money, as well as your dreams, aspirations and goals for the future.

> Understanding issues such as personal behavioral biases, compensation differences, and fiduciary standards will help you make a wise choice in selecting a competent professional financial advisor.

An advisor who prioritizes these important factors will ask you questions about your values and/or offer assessments to better understand your financial perspective. If you do not feel comfortable sharing personal information, move along until you find an advisor you trust and look forward to talking to. If it is difficult discussing such matters, find an advisor who has the patience to allow you to develop the trust necessary to move forward in a productive way.

Questions to Ask Your Advisor

1. Are you acting as my fiduciary? Will you sign an agreement
   stating you are acting as my fiduciary at all times?
   *This is the most important question of all. Ask this before even
   scheduling an initial meeting. If the advisor will not act as your
   legal fiduciary or sign such an agreement, keep looking.*

2. Do you have a way to measure the value your clients receive
   in relationship to the fees paid?
   *Can the advisor show you annually if you are on track for
   meeting your individual financial planning goals? An advisor
   who can only show you performance based on the rate of
   return relative to an index may not be your best choice. This
   tells you nothing about how well you are achieving your goals.*

3. Do you have any affiliation with a broker-dealer?
   *An advisor with a broker-dealer affiliation (other than a
   custodial arrangement) is a registered representative and in the
   business of sales. This is not your best choice.*

4. Do you use a third-party custodian, such as Charles Schwab,
   TD Ameritrade or Fidelity to hold my assets?
   *The fee-only advisor should have an outside custodian. Common
   custodians are the companies above. The custodian generates
   separate account statements and holds your assets safe. If your
   advisor is generating his own statement of your investments
   and you do not get trade confirmations from a separate source,
   I would seriously consider finding a new advisor, quickly.*

5. Who is your ideal client?

   Does his ideal client sound like you … or not?

6. What is your fee structure? How are you compensated?

   You want to look for an advisor who is fee-only and accepts no commissions or kickbacks. You also want to consider an advisor who accepts a separate fee for financial planning. If the fee for financial planning is included in the percentage charged to manage the investment assets, make sure the financial plan covers the financial planning areas important to you, such as financial position, protection planning, investments, retirement planning, tax planning, and estate planning.

7. Do you get additional compensation or financial incentives for recommending certain investments or referring me to an insurance provider, attorney, CPA, or other referral?

   If the answer is yes, learn more, or keep looking.

8. What are your qualifications and experience?

   Minimum financial qualification should be a CERTIFIED FINANCIAL PLANNER® (CFP®).

9. Will you be the only person working with me?

   If the advisor works in teams, ask yourself if you feel comfortable with the other advisors. Determine how you will know whom to call when.

10. Who owns your company?

   Is the firm owned by a big conglomerate—bank, brokerage, venture capital firm? Ask about potential conflicts of interest and how he will make sure to put your needs above those of the firm's owners.

11. Do you have clients who might be willing to speak with me about your services?

Although advisors should be respectful of client confidentiality, they also should be willing to give you a list of names of clients similar to you.

12. Do you have an account minimum?

Minimums can be as low as $100,000 or as high as $10+ million. Minimums of $500,000 to $1 million are common. Typically, fee-only firms charge between 1 to 1.5 percent per year of assets managed and reductions for larger balances.

CHAPTER 4

FINANCIAL PLANNING:
THE CRUCIAL FIRST STEP TO INVESTMENT SUCCESS

Planning is bringing the future into the present

so that you can do something about it now.

—ALAN LAKEIN

Let our advance worrying become

advance thinking and planning.

—WINSTON CHURCHILL

If you don't know your destination, how will you know how to get there and when you've arrived?

As a child, my family went on several road trips. Before we left, Mom would call the American Automobile Association (AAA) and obtain a step-by-step map of our planned route. The map would highlight the danger zones, construction sites and slow areas, and plot the fastest way to get to our destination. Today, our mobile phones can deliver routes via GPS, talking to us throughout the trip, and estimating the time of arrival.

A financial plan works the same way as a road map or GPS. Without a destination, direction, or goal, it's easy to go nowhere. A financial plan helps you identify your destination, in other words, how much money you will need to meet your retirement goals, education savings, or estate-planning objectives. A plan will also help you understand the potential roadblocks and if any gaps exist between your envisioned destination and the reality of getting there. Ask yourself this:

What money directions are you interested in taking?
Where are you lacking direction?

I know, I know ... it's easy to put off financial planning. It's easy to let day-to-day activities get in the way of sitting down and thinking about your life goals and financial situation. A Prudential Financial study points out the two most common roadblocks to financial planning:

1. Thirty-six percent of married women indicate that "the immediate needs of my family/children take priority (over financial planning)."

2. Thirty-four percent of those nearing retirement say, "I'm afraid I'll make the wrong decision, so I tend to avoid thinking about financial planning."

If you've been putting off financial planning, start now, start today. Do not let worry, procrastination, or inaction affect your ability to finally have the peace of mind necessary to make intelligent decisions. There is no downside to financial planning, but there is a multitude of upsides.

In a survey by the Financial Planning Association, people with a professionally developed financial plan were three times as likely to feel "very" or "extremely" prepared for retirement, versus people with no financial advisor support. The same study found that people benefited most when their financial advisor developed a comprehensive financial plan instead of merely providing advice on specific investments. Investors with professionally prepared plans were significantly more likely to say they:

- felt more in control of their financial futures;

- were on track to meet goals of retirement planning, college funding, and adequate protection;

- were better prepared for unexpected events because they made cash reserves and emergency funds a priority;

> Am I heading in the right direction? I feel relief in knowing I'm on track.

- had an optimistic outlook about their future, even during market downturns; and

- had a greater depth of understanding about financial issues and their own financial activities.

What is a Financial Plan?

Financial planning is the process of determining your primary financial and life goals, whether you can achieve them based on your current financial picture, and how your financial strategy might need to change over time in order to meet those goals. Financial planning takes the uncertainty out of your financial future by helping you answer this basic question:

What size nest egg will provide the income
you need during retirement to meet your monthly expenses
and not run out of money?

Until you know this number, no amount of investment return will provide the comfort you need to plan securely for the future.

Unfortunately, traditional financial planning is a data-driven process that doesn't take into account an individual's temperament and life goals. Sure, many advisors say they do financial planning. In reality, most are producing plans that address only a small piece of your financial life—a list of investments, for example, or an assets-and-liabilities spreadsheet.

Additionally, a successful retirement depends upon a lot more than money. A simple balance sheet listing your investments is meaningless unless you know how to measure how well those assets will help you achieve your goals—financially and in life.

Will your money help you buy a second home?

Will it help fund your kids' education?

Will you have enough to retire early and teach English abroad or join the Peace Corps?

In addition to helping you achieve your dreams, a solid financial plan can also help you weather unexpected negative events such as a job loss, divorce, disability, or death of a spouse. By helping you prepare for the unexpected, a financial plan can reduce feelings of vulnerability and allow you to move toward the future with confidence and clarity.

Getting Down to Specifics

Financial planning is among the most multifaceted and complicated disciplines for financial advisors to master. A successful advisor must not only have extensive knowledge about the financial planning process, they must also know how to apply the knowledge to your particular situation. This requires a thorough understanding of your goals, attitudes, and personal preferences.

Advisors with this broad knowledge will be able to help you maintain your standard of living during retirement, become economically self-sufficient, minimize your taxes on retirement distributions, and understand Medicare and Social Security. They can also help you address specific financial issues, such as covering unexpected healthcare costs, making charitable contributions, caring for dependent parents, supplementing your grandchildren's education, and updating estate and beneficiary documents.

When developing a financial plan, qualified professional advisors will work with you to understand such things as: how long you want to work, what your prospects are for health and longevity, whether you are disciplined to save enough for retirement, and to what extent you are willing to accept investment risks. Additionally, they will address how family dynamics, financial behavior, and money messages learned during childhood might support or hinder your objectives.

By taking all of this information into account when creating a financial plan, your advisor will help you see the choices you are making about retirement every day.

Too many have vague ideas about how they want to spend their later years, but those ideas are not specific or measurable. An important element in financial planning is *naming* and *quantifying* your goals and, where necessary, distinguishing those goals from dreams. There is a simple "acid test" to determine whether a desired financial outcome is a dream or a goal. It involves a two-part question:

1. Are you *willing* to do whatever is necessary to accomplish your goal?

   If you are willing to do whatever is necessary, you will make an unwavering commitment to realizing the goal, no matter how difficult, how long it takes, or how much personal sacrifice is required.

2. Are you *able* to do whatever is necessary to accomplish your goal?

   Being able to do what is necessary means that you have the capability, talent, and resources to achieve your ambitions— but you may or may not be willing to put those capabilities to work.

If you answered "no" to either of the acid-test questions, if you are not willing or able to do what is necessary to achieve your goals, then you are not planning, you are dreaming. Although dreaming is an important first step, the financial advisor's role is to help convert your vague dreams into specific goals that can be measured—and achieved.

For some, retirement is the time when work is entirely optional, when there are sufficient resources to sustain their chosen lifestyle. This is the traditional retirement paradigm. But there are other "retirement" options. Some may choose or need to work full or part-time later in life, going in

> Aging is not lost youth, but a new stage of opportunity and strength.
> —BETTY FRIEDAN

and out of the workforce. Others may use the retirement years to find new ways to be productive, contributing members of society well into their advanced age.

Know Thyself

This fact is so important it bears repeating: the most effective financial advisors go beyond traditional data-driven financial planning and help you understand your natural behavior around money, how you make decisions, what you want in life, and how money can help you make smart and confident choices about retirement.

The only way to know what is best for you—both financially and in life—is by understanding your goals, emotions, and values around money.

Think about it. Do you view money as a way to gain security? Independence? Power? Respect? Is money a means to a particular lifestyle? Do discussions about money make you anxious? A financial plan designed with your particular temperament in mind increases the likelihood you will stick with the plan.

As you begin the planning process, ask yourself:

> *What is my financial vision twenty years from now?*
> *What do I want for myself and my family?*

Think about your ideal life and what you want to do upon retirement?

> *Are you interested in pursuing a second career, developing a hobby, starting a business, sailing, volunteering, or golfing?*
> *Whom do you want to spend time with?*
> *How do you intend to stay healthy and active?*

Too many have vague ideas about how they want to spend their later years, but those ideas are not specific or measurable.

A successful retirement is one in which you are living the way you want to live—and money is the means to get there.

See the Appendix for Your Financial Planning Philosophy— seven critical questions that will refocus your life around money.

Questions to Ask Your Advisor:

1. Do you provide a comprehensive financial plan?

   Do you have a sample I can look at?

   A comprehensive plan covers the six elements of a solid financial plan: Financial Position, Protection Planning, Investments, Retirement Planning, Tax Planning, and Estate Planning.

2. What do you charge for developing a financial plan?

   If there is no charge, ask to see a sample of a financial plan to see if it covers the six key planning areas. More often than not, if there is no charge, the advisor will have only created an investment plan—not a financial plan.

3. What is your financial planning process?

   Ask your advisor how they will get the information necessary to understand what is important to you. If they only have you complete a form (without also interviewing you or engaging you in conversation), they may be missing a critical discovery that incorporates right-brain creative thinking. Both creative right-brain and tactical left-brain approaches are necessary for long-term investment success.

4. What information do you need to complete the financial plan?

   Make sure your advisor's information-gathering process is comprehensive and includes such things as completing a behavioral assessment and uncovering your goals and values, in addition to reviewing your insurance policies, tax returns, and estate-planning documents.

5. What is the estimated time frame for completion of the financial plan?

Six to eight weeks is about the standard time needed to complete a comprehensive plan.

6. How often do you update the plan?

Annually is ideal for a financial plan, although you may want to meet or talk quarterly to review and discuss other areas of planning.

7. Do you help implement the financial plan? Do you receive compensation from the referral or the product?

The expectation is that your advisor will help implement the plan in all of the six areas by working with your accountant, attorney, insurance provider, and others to make sure your plan gets on track. Your advisor should receive no compensation for referring you and no commission for suggesting a product. This is why you pay a separate financial planning fee.

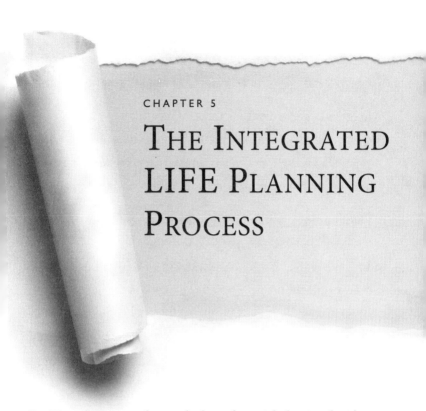

CHAPTER 5

THE INTEGRATED LIFE PLANNING PROCESS

Now that you understand what a financial plan is, why it's necessary, and how it differs from a more straightforward investment plan, let's look at how financial planning influences investment planning and what financial and investment planning look like as an integrated process. For shorthand purposes, let's call this integrated process Life Planning.

Ideally, your advisor should take you through a comprehensive life planning process that includes four stages: Discover, Design, Make Good and Grow.

1. Discover – Gather information and prioritize goals

In the discovery phase of financial planning, tools are used to help you discover your goals, attitudes, values and preferences. This step should be designed to reveal the unique "you," including how you feel about your past, present and future.

In order to understand your current financial situation and goals, your advisor will likely request certain documentation from you, such as employer benefits summaries, tax returns, insurance policies, monthly spending data, and financial statements.

But the advisor should not stop there. He should take the time to understand your broader predispositions for spending, saving and goal-setting. Hugh Massie with DNA Behavior International believes that the financial planning life cycle is, first and foremost, about managing and understanding financial *behavioral* biases. He describes this as "understanding people before numbers."

Massie's belief in understanding people before numbers is backed up by research by Meir Statman that indicates a whopping 93.6 percent of the success of an individual's financial plan is related to the investor's emotions and behavior, e.g., temperament, past experiences, communication style, and only 6.4 percent of success is related to actual investment performance.

In short, behavior drives financial planning performance, and a successful plan is one that takes into account your personality and how you relate to money. Consequently, the financial planning process needs to consider both left-brain linear thinking (which is financially focused) and right-brain creative thinking (which focuses on temperament, personality, and needs).

Your chosen financial advisor will need to understand your attitudes, beliefs, and values about money—on both conscious and subconscious levels because they all influence your financial decisions. For example, if you are a big-picture person focused on creating a quality lifestyle, you may prefer financial meetings to be fun and open and include colorful graphics. If you are a person focused on stability, your advisor should address your concerns about security. If you do best with detailed information, the advisor should provide analysis and research. If you are a goal-setter, you will likely want your advisor to get to the point, focus on opportunities and allow for discussion.

If your advisor does not understand these natural tendencies, he or she won't be able to create a plan that addresses your likely reactions in both up and down markets. A successful plan will help you avoid such reactiveness by helping you become aware of your beliefs and incorporating them into your plan. (A side benefit of becoming aware of your beliefs about money: it can help you develop healthier attitudes toward money.)

In addition to gathering data and uncovering your behavioral

> Take a free communications assessment to understand your behavioral biases around financial information at *WealthLegacyInstitute.com*.

biases, the discovery process should provide a way for you to explore your ideal future. For instance, is saving on taxes or buying a second home within ten years more important to you? Do you want to travel upon retirement or move to Costa Rica? What about expanding your business? Giving to worthy causes? Taking regular vacations? Spending more time with family? Which, if any, of these goals is important to you? Make sure your advisor understands your goals and how you prioritize them.

2. Design – Analyze the information

Once your advisor has gathered your financial documents and assessed your behavioral and communication biases, he or she will be ready to develop an overall picture of your income, expenses, and net worth. Then, the advisor can begin to evaluate potential planning gaps or issues that could prevent you from achieving your retirement objectives. Typical planning gaps include such things as erratic cash flow, lack of a financial tracking system, too much risk, poor asset location, insufficient tax planning, and an inability to rebalance the portfolio on a regular basis.

> This health issue really scared us; it helped me prioritize my values. I can no longer work the mad hours I've been doing. We need a plan, so I can return to work with a sense of power and know when I tell them I will not work those hours or I choose to work part-time, I'll know the impact on our future.

Armed with a comprehensive understanding of your current financial picture as well as an analysis of the potential issues, the advisor can begin to work with you to make decisions about the design and direction of your plan. The design step, in short, should include a thorough review of the options, benefits, costs, and risks associated with each potential course of action.

3. Make Good – Put the plan to work

Once the data analysis is complete, you can begin to work with your advisor to put your financial plan to work. When you implement your strategies, you are: accumulating resources for financial security later; preserving your money so that it lasts as long as needed; and/or deciding how to transfer your assets to the next generation or others through succession planning.

Implementation is the most important step of the financial planning process. After all, a financial plan that is not implemented provides little value.

Depending on your individual plan, specific action items related to implementation might include:

- Calling your insurance broker to adjust policy deductibles or eliminate physical damage coverage on older cars

- Increasing the yield on cash reserves

- Consolidating bank or investment accounts

- Reducing costs on your insurance protection

> Am I heading in the right direction? I need relief in knowing I'm on track.

- Contributing to a 529 plan

- Adjusting your investment portfolio to recalibrate your risk tolerance

- Changing W-2 tax withholding

- Changing the allocation on your 401(k)

- Increasing your contribution to a Roth IRA

- Meeting with an attorney to complete your estate planning documents.

4. Grow – Monitor the plan

The entire purpose of creating a financial plan is to ensure that your short (3–5 years), intermediate (6–10 years), and long-term (over 10 years) goals are met. Thus, it's essential to monitor the plan on a regular basis to make sure your portfolio is growing and that you're on track to meet your goals. Regular review and management of the plan enables your financial advisor to determine your progress and make adjustments based on economic, financial, and life events.

This structured, ongoing management is the money secret that allows you to feel confident and in control of your financial situation, regardless of the changes and challenges.

A Case Study in Life Planning

Martha and Steve had enjoyed a 40-year marriage that began in their early 20s. Within two years of Steve retiring from a Fortune 100 company, he died. After his death, their adult children believed Martha to be sitting on a pile of money gained from insurance proceeds and the distribution of Steve's stock options and grants. Because of this, the children began to make a series of significant financial requests—underwriting the grandkids' private schools tuitions, seeding a start-up business, paying the mortgage on a house. Because Martha loved and wanted to support her family, she began writing her children checks as needed.

Because of these checks, within two years, Martha's secure nest egg had declined by 25 percent. Although she and her husband had planned for their retirement, her financial future was now seriously at risk.

To get Martha back on track, the bleeding had to stop. It was time to review and renew the elements of her financial plan.

At Wealth Legacy Institute, we took Martha through a comprehensive planning process involving the four steps discussed in this chapter. We call our process Planning for LIFE Experience™.

Here's what the process looked like.

DISCOVER:

During the discovery process, we gathered the data and documentation necessary to understand Martha's current financial situation. (We had already completed an extensive financial review when her husband was alive, but the information had to be updated.)

Our discovery process also revealed that Martha had a natural tendency to give to others, and that her primary goals in life were stability and keeping her family happy. Unfortunately, her generosity and desire for family happiness were at odds with her need for retirement stability. Furthermore, her husband had always handled their investments, and because of this, she frequently felt incompetent around money.

In recognizing these things about herself, it became clear to Martha that although her family was important, her financial security was far more critical than taking care of her adult children—especially because she didn't want to become a burden to them later.

Martha was now ready to get her financial plan back on track by putting her financial needs first and educating herself about the planning process and financial terminology.

DESIGN:

We designed a financial plan that helped Martha make decisions about her future by reviewing different options. If she continued granting money requests to her children, the plan showed that her assets would be depleted by age 85. Not only that, the probability of her retirement staying on track plummeted from 99 percent to just 68 percent. In looking at the plan, it became clear to Martha that although she had depleted some of her nest egg, she would still be able to live the lifestyle important to her as long as she made a few modifications. (We brainstormed with her to decide what these modifications would be.)

Knowing that she could still live the life she wanted, her fears about her financial future evaporated. However, Martha was still extremely nervous about telling her children that she could no longer financially help them.

MAKE GOOD:

In order for Martha to implement the plan, she had to confront her children. Because she was nervous about this, Martha agreed for us to schedule a family meeting in our office. At the meeting, Martha shared her heartfelt conflict between wanting to help her children and meet her own long-term needs.

With Martha's permission, we shared the detailed results of her financial plan with her children, and they immediately understood their mother's position. Clarity surfaced. Her children

Stages	Value	Commitment	Time
Discover	Clarity	Discovery Meeting: • Communication DNA • Natural Behavior DNA • Values Clarification • Humanigraphix™	1-2 Hours
Design	Decisions	Data Gathering Meeting: • Financial Position Organizer	2-4 Hours
Make Good	Results	Financial Plan Review Meeting: • Plan Implementation	1-2 Hours
Grow	Confidence	Annual or Quarterly Meetings: • Goal Prioritization • Investment Strategy • Retirement Plan Review • Tax Strategy	1 Hour

realized if they continued to take their mother's money, she would run out and they might have to care for her.

In that meeting, a joint decision was made that no one would make any more financial requests of Martha.

GROW:

We were able to continuously monitor—and revise—Martha's plan as her needs shifted and her experience of not giving became part of her new lifestyle. Not giving to her kids was not easy on Martha. Her relationship with her children and grandchildren meant everything to her.

Based on this ongoing discomfort, we worked with Martha to carve out a specific dollar amount to give to each adult child as an early "inheritance" to use as needed—but made it clear no more would be forthcoming. In doing this, the children received an unexpected windfall, and Martha felt thrilled to be able to give in such a fair and consistent way.

We also repositioned her investment assets to eliminate certain tax consequences, and we reviewed long-term care options and helped her decide which policy to purchase in order to reduce the possibility of becoming a burden to her family later.

The confidence Martha acquired by getting her LIFE Plan back on track helped her feel secure once again.

Six Key Elements of a Solid Financial Plan

1. Balance Sheet
- monthly income versus monthly expenses
- discretionary income
- cash reserve levels
- net worth
- lines of credit

2. Insurance
- health care
- long-term care timing/premiums
- property and casualty
- life insurance
- disability options

3. Investments
- asset allocation
- risk tolerance
- stock funds, bond funds, cash
- diversification strategies
- cost basis—tax implications

4. Retirement
- required minimum distributions (RMD)
- pre-59½ strategies
- Medicare/Medigap
- Social Security
- 401(k), IRA, Roth conversions

5. Tax Strategy
- tax reduction
- tax deferral
- tax avoidance
- effects of liquidation
- gifting

6. Estate Plan
- wills, trusts, asset ownership
- estate balancing and capital transfer
- business succession
- charitable planning
- beneficiary identification

Questions for Your Advisor to Ask You:

All six key elements are interrelated. There is not one decision in one planning area that does not affect another. Selling a particular stock fund, for example, may incur capital gains taxes. Deciding to supplement your parents' care may affect the amount you can set aside for your child's college education, delay your desired retirement date, or both.

Understanding the information your advisor needs to create a solid life plan will help you prepare for the discovery process. Here is a list of some of the questions your advisor should ask during the discovery process.

1. To help create your balance sheet, your advisor should ask questions like:

   - What do you feel is standing in the way of improving your cash flow?

   - What is preventing you from saving on a regular basis?

   - What amount of discretionary income exists monthly?

   - How would you cope with a sudden financial emergency (like a job loss), or if you needed to help a family member?

   - If you could change just one thing about your current financial position, what would it be? Why is that important to you?

2. To help determine your insurance needs, your advisor should ask questions like:

- How likely is it that you might become a caregiver for a loved one?

- Have you talked with your parents, in-laws, or husband/partner about needing or giving long-term care?

- Should a family member require care, what plans do you currently have in place?

- Where do you plan to retire? What are the costs of home care, assisted living, and nursing homes in that area?

- How familiar are you with what funding the government does and does not provide when it comes to long-term care?

- Do you have a family history of Alzheimer's or diabetes?

- Do you think you will have enough to pay for quality care and have enough retirement income?

- If you were to lose your spouse/partner tomorrow, what would you do? Would you change your lifestyle? Would you return to work? Would you move?

- When was the last review of your life insurance premiums and projections?

3. To help determine your investment plan, your advisor should work with you to determine the answers to the following questions:

- How much do you plan to set aside monthly or in a lump sum to achieve your goal?

- What is your target rate of return on the investments for your goal? How did you determine your targeted rate of return?

- How will inflation affect your goal?

- What effect will taxes have on your goal?

4. To help your advisor create a solid retirement plan, be prepared to answer questions like:

- What does retirement mean to you?

- What do you see yourself doing? Will you work? Will you travel?

- What should we budget in your plan for travel or hobbies?

- What concerns you most about retirement?

- What might get in the way?

- How could healthcare costs and taxes affect your retirement security?

- Who might you need to take care of—spouse, parents, children—later in life?

- What have you done so far to secure your retirement? Do you think it will be enough?

5. To help determine the appropriate tax strategy for your situation, you advisor should be asking questions like:

- How do you feel about the taxes you pay?

- What concerns you most about your tax situation?

- What have you done to reduce your taxes?

- Do you usually get a refund or owe income taxes?

- How has your earned income changed over the last five years? What do you see in the next five years?

- How do you use your taxable interest and dividend income? Is it needed for income, reinvested for growth, or another purpose? (Schedule B)

- Tell me about the terms of your divorce agreement. How long will you receive (or pay) alimony?

- How long have you been in business? Where do you see your business in five years? (Schedule C or C-EZ)

- What are your thoughts about the capital gains taxes you are paying? Do you have unused capital losses? (Schedule D)

- How long have you been a landlord? What are the plans for the property? (Schedule E)

- What strategies are you using to reduce the impact of taxes on your Social Security benefits?

- How have your itemized deductions changed in the last five years? (Schedule A)

- How do you feel about AMT (Alternative Minimum Tax)? (Form 6251)

- Would it be all right if I contacted your accountant to discuss your financial plan?

- Do you think you are doing all you can to reduce your taxes?

6. To help you create an estate plan that reflects your individual values and monetary situation, your advisor should be asking questions like:

- What values would you like to make sure that you pass on to your family?

- What do you know about federal and state laws that affect your estate?

- What are your plans to pass assets to your family, charity, or both?

- What have you done so far to ensure your legacy plans are carried out?

- Do you have a will, trust, ethical will? When were your documents drafted?

- Do you own property in another state? What is the structure of ownership?

CHAPTER 6

DEBUNKING THE BIGGEST INVESTMENT MYTH

All the time and effort people devote to picking the right fund, the hot hand, the great manager, have in most cases led to no advantage.

—PETER LYNCH,
Fidelity Magellan Fund Manager, 1977 to 1990

Most investors, both institutional and individual, will find that the best way to own common stocks is through an index fund that charges minimal fees.

—WARREN E. BUFFETT,
Chairman and CEO, Berkshire Hathaway, Inc.

Many investors believe that beating the stock market or an appropriate benchmark is the be-all and end-all goal of investing. If the market rises 6 percent, they want 9. If the market leaps 18 percent, they hunger for 20. You get these extraordinary returns, they say, through effort and active management: watching stocks daily, buying on the potential rise, selling before the decline, picking the next hot stock, or owning actively managed mutual funds. Sit back and wait for the market to grow over time? Not a chance. Active investing is where it's at.

With all due respect to active investors, continuously beating the market year after year is simply not possible. The only sure thing about active investing is that you'll make significantly less money over time. In fact, the idea that you can beat the market through active investing may well be the biggest investment myth out there. The best way to grow wealth is by taking a more passive—I call it patient—approach to investing.

> My preferred financial behavior is simply denial.

Let me explain.

The investment world is filled with financial advisors and fund managers who actively monitor the market and make investment decisions daily based on their projection of where the market is heading. If they believe the market will drop, they'll sell stock to preserve an investment. If they believe a stock is headed up, they'll buy more to get while the gettin' is good. The key word here is believe. These advisors don't actually know where a particular stock is heading at any given time. All that buying and selling activity is based on forecasting what they think might happen.

Sure, occasionally stock pickers guess right and make money for their clients. But more often than not, active managers and active investors fail to outperform the market. Case in point: the vast majority—between 62 and 78 percent—of actively managed funds failed to outperform the market in years between 2007 and 2014.

The Failure of Active Management, 2007–2014

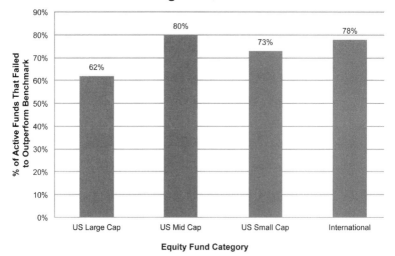

Source: Wealth Legacy Institute

Because financial professionals such as fund managers and investment advisors are often evaluated based on how well they do relative to the market overall, they are motivated to continually buy and sell. But individual investors also fall prey to the active-investing mindset. If you've ever bought stock based on a tip from a co-worker, or called your advisor to sell a fund because of a magazine article, you've actively invested—and in the process, likely decreased your potential for long-term gain.

How to Find—and Avoid—Active Investors

The financial world is filled with active investors. They can be found in a variety of establishments:

- At mutual fund companies such as Putnam, MFS, Legg Mason, Eaton Vance, Franklin Templeton, Janus, Fidelity, Columbia, and Van Kampen, to name just a few. Fund managers in actively managed funds aim to outperform a specific stock market index such as the S&P 500 or the Russell 2000. Fund managers active trading expenses decrease your rate of return potential and therefore decrease your potential for long-term growth.

- In traditional retail brokerage firms such as Morgan Stanley, Merrill Lynch, UBS, and Wells Fargo Advisors, many brokers trade on their clients' behalf.

- At consumer retail brokerage firms like Scottrade, Edward Jones and Charles Schwab, which have opened storefronts to *sell* product to investors so that consumers can trade.

- Inside third-party institutional custodians such as TD Ameritrade, Charles Schwab, or Fidelity. Fee-only financial fiduciaries use these custodians to keep your money safe inside a separate account under your name. In that capacity, these custodians are fine. But be aware that these third-party custodians also act as broker-dealers that sell directly to the public—and in that capacity, they are in the business of *sales* and are not acting as your fiduciary.

Day traders, market timers, and options traders also focus on active investing. In fact, the number of active investors in the market overall is growing three times faster than the number of patient investors, according to Celent, a market research firm. This is because brokerage firms and other companies that profit from increased trading encourage this behavior through advertising.

> Learning about investing from a non-fiduciary financial institution is like trying to learn about eating healthy from the fast food industry.

Even fee-only financial fiduciaries can get drawn into the active-investing cycle, often because clients think active trading is what investing is all about. It's not.

Growing your wealth is what investing is about.

The High Cost of Active Investing

There are many reasons active investing—by you, your financial advisor, or a manager—will cost you money in the long run. They fall into two main categories:

- *Higher costs:* Active investing costs more than passive investing because of trade fees, sales commissions on mutual funds, closing costs, and an array of hidden fees built in to cover the cost of analysts and economists.

- *Unpredictable markets:* When it comes right down to it, no one can consistently beat the market year after year. Active investors try to time their investments to avoid losses and capture gains, but they end up missing out on gains and locking in losses because the stock market is inherently unpredictable.

Given all the research that suggests active stock trading is a loser's game, why is there such emphasis on active trading? Because that's what managers inside financial services firms—which spend close to $10 billion a year in advertising in financial media such as *Fortune, Money* magazine, and *CBS Money Watch*—want you to believe. If investors knew the money secret that active investing was useless, much of the personal financial media—including online investing sites—would cease to exist.

Brokers get you to override your common sense by appealing to your emotions and your sense of self. In particular, they know most of us think of ourselves as smarter than average. "Because you're smarter than the average investor," they'll tell you, "you shouldn't settle for an investment that merely provides average returns. You need a manager who has an active strategy for beating the market."

The problem is that these active brokers are choosing to ignore another money secret: that dozens of academic studies reveal how rare it is that active managers actually beat the market. Worse yet, these brokers also neglect to share this money secret: that actively traded funds have above-average expenses and

above-average trading costs that you will have to pay regardless
of the fund's success or failure.

The Low Cost of Passive Investing

Passive investing is a management style where a fund's portfolio
return mirrors a market index. By investing in an index fund
designed to replicate a particular market, such as the Dow Jones
Industrial Average (30 blue chip stocks), the Standard & Poor's
500 (American companies valued at more than $10 billion), the
Russell 2000 (the 2000 smallest publicly traded companies),
or the Aggregate Bond Index (the entire US bond market), an
investor reaps the results of that
index, minus costs, through the
total combined performance of the
entire market.

> I do not trust myself. I sold
> out at the bottom and now
> must work to recover.

Index funds are as close to foolproof investing as you can get
because the return of the index over time relatively matches the
overall market for that index. If, on the other hand, you purchase
an actively managed fund, your return likely will be below average.

Patient Investing™
The Empowered Pathway to Wealth

Eugene Fama, widely recognized as the father of modern finance,
won the Nobel Prize in Economics for his Efficient Market
Hypothesis, which implies that stock prices are extremely difficult

to predict in the short run, and that all available information relating to a company's financial health is quickly incorporated into prices. The notion that there are experts who understand where the market is heading is false.

Markets are more efficient than active investors for one reason: active investors are vulnerable to behavioral bias such as over-confidence and overreaction, both of which cost money. Given that markets are impossible to beat through forecasting over the long run, your goal as an investor should be to own the market by becoming a *Patient Investor*™.

Patient Investors avoid subjective short-term forecasts (by brokers, analysts, economists, media, co-workers, etc.). Instead, they take a long-term view by owning a globally diversified portfolio of passively managed type funds. This allows them to capture positive performance when it occurs without incurring expensive ongoing sales and trading charges.

The Active Hunter Versus the Patient Farmer

One way to understand patient investing is to think about the difference between a hunter and a farmer. A hunter goes into the forest looking for an opportunity to capture its prey. The excitement and uncertainty of the hunt fuels his willingness to risk. He thrives on the adrenalin. He's active at all times. The problem with hunting is that the hunter often comes home with nothing.

A farmer, on the other hand, plants a field of crops, carefully and patiently tends the soil, and waits for nature to take its course. Wall Street wants the hunters who crave emotional stimulation and quick hits of adrenalin and are willing to hand over their money to get it. Patient farmers are too practical for Wall Street's tastes.

One of the primary methods of Patient Investing™ is using a hybrid of indexing.

Patient Investing provides a number of benefits over active investing, including:

- **Consistency**: Patient Investing provides more consistent and reliable returns because there is no active (or, more accurately, reactive) manager making investment mistakes based on emotion.

- **Control**: With Patient Investing, you and your financial advisor can work together to create a customized and diversified mix of passive-like funds that meet the needs of your particular situation. Active mutual fund managers, by comparison, choose stocks that meet the fund's needs— not yours.

- **Lower cost**: Patient Investing is cheaper than actively managed funds because index funds don't incur the costs associated with never-ending stock trades, nor do they have to cover the salaries of active fund managers and other experts. In the past, funds with the lowest expenses have typically delivered the highest net returns.

> If investors knew the money secret that active investing was useless, much of the personal financial media—including online investing sites—would cease to exist.

Assume 6.5% Annualized Return Chart

Source: Wealth Legacy Institute

Cost Matters

Over time, high mutual fund fees, sales commissions, and other expenses associated with actively managed funds can be a significant drag on wealth creation. As the graph illustrates, at a 6.5 percent rate of return, an investment of $1 million with a management fee of 1 percent returns almost $5 million over thirty years. By contrast, the same $1 million investment with total fees of three percent will generate $2 million *less*.

Questions to Ask Your Advisor

To find an advisor who takes a patient approach to investing, ask your current or potential advisor these questions:

1. Would you define yourself as an active or passive investor?
   Look for a passive, or patient investor™.

2. Can you provide empirical evidence that your active approach to investing will beat the market over the long term?
   It is impossible for anyone to provide this kind of evidence. If an advisor suggests this is possible, walk away.

3. What types of investments do you use?
   Look for an advisor who utilizes low-cost, passive-type funds.

4. Do you use a select group of mutual funds? Do you receive any financial benefit from those mutual fund companies, including payment for travel, entertainment, workshops, client events and the like?
   You do not want to hire an advisor who accepts any financial favors from mutual fund companies.

5. What other fees exist in my portfolio, such as 12b-1 fees, fee-sharing arrangements, rebates, service charges, mark-ups, trade fees, surrender fees, custody fees, and more? Will you break down the total amount of fees paid in each portfolio or show me in the fund's prospectus?

It's easy for fee-only financial fiduciaries to detail the fees and costs associated with managing your portfolio. Always look at total costs when evaluating portfolios.

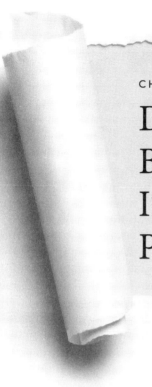

CHAPTER 7

DIVERSIFY TO BUILD A STURDY INVESTMENT PLAN

Diversification is a strategy that can be summed up by the timeless adage: "Don't put all your eggs in one basket."

—Unknown

Have you ever noticed that street vendors often sell seemingly unrelated products, such as umbrellas and sunscreen? Initially, that may seem odd. When would a person buy both at the same time? Probably never—and that's the point. Street vendors know that when it is raining, it is easier to sell umbrellas but harder to sell sunscreen. When it is sunny, the reverse is true. By offering both items, the vendor is diversifying the product line in order to reduce the risk of losing money on any given day.

This same strategy—diversifying the product line—is exactly what successful investors do. Instead of buying stock in a company that only sells umbrellas, or buying stock in a company that only sells sunscreen, or locking up all their money in bank accounts, smart investors balance their bets by diversifying their investments. This way, if the value of one investment drops, the investor has other investments to offset the decline.

> My broker had me in all stocks. During the last recession, I lost a huge amount of money.

How to Diversify
Step One:
Understand the Risks and Your Ability to Tolerate Risk

In the financial world, investments are most often diversified three ways—among stocks, bonds, and cash—all of which have different risk profiles. Stocks are the riskiest investment because although they can realize tremendous gains, they also can suffer tremendous losses. Bonds are less risky than stocks, but still carry some level of risk. Cash is considered the safest investment, but the potential for gain is also limited. In short, if the potential for loss (and growth) is high, an investment is considered risky; if the potential for loss (and growth) is low, so is the risk.

As an investor, your portfolio should be tailored to the level of risk you are willing to assume based on your age, temperament, financial situation, and life goals. Since it's impossible to have a low risk of loss and a high rate of return, you have to decide which trade-offs you are willing to make.

The most important and most difficult decision you will make as an investor is deciding your level of risk tolerance. Unfortunately, most investors are poor judges of their ability to tolerate risk. When the stock market is up, investors rate their risk tolerance as high, but when prices and values are dropping, they feel more conservative. Although there are many online tools available to help determine risk tolerance, none of them are comprehensive enough to help individuals and couples understand all the financial and emotional factors that contribute to a person's ability to tolerate risk.

It's difficult to know your risk-tolerance level without conducting an assessment of your risk capacity. To help determine your risk capacity, you need to conduct a thorough review of your short-term needs and the time horizon, net income, net worth, risk attitude, and investment knowledge. This is why the financial planning process discussed earlier is such a crucial first step toward investment success. Unless you know the financial goals you wish to achieve—and by when—it's extremely difficult to determine your overall risk profile, in other words, where you fall on the spectrum between being a low-risk or high-risk investor.

To help you determine your risk tolerance, your advisor should give you one or more behavioral assessments. The results will help you understand the appropriate asset allocation for your portfolio.

What Type of Investor Are You?

Low-risk tolerance investors

Low-risk tolerance investors prefer knowing their capital is safe, and they're not comfortable investing in equities. They would rather keep their money in the bank. Low-risk investors are unlikely to have much experience with investing beyond bank accounts. They typically suffer severe regret if their decisions turn out poorly. Low-risk investors with time horizons of ten years or more typically have portfolios with a majority of bonds and cash, with little exposure to equities or other higher-risk investments. Low-risk investors need to understand that their caution can mean their investments may not keep pace with inflation, or they may fail to meet their investment goals.

Low-to-mid-risk tolerance investors

Investors with low-to-mid-risk tolerance would prefer not to take risks with their investments, but they may do so to a limited extent. They would prefer to keep their money in the bank, but they realize other investments might be better over the long term. Low-to-mid-risk investors may have some limited experience with investments, but they are more familiar with bank accounts than other types of investments. Low-to-mid-risk investors can often suffer regret when decisions turn out poorly. Low-to-mid-risk investors with time horizons of ten or more years typically have portfolios with a majority of bonds and cash, but with some exposure to equities and other higher-risk investments.

Mid-risk tolerance investors

Mid-risk tolerance investors understand that they have to take on some investment risks to meet their long-term goals. They're often more willing to take risk with at least part of their available assets. Mid-risk investors may have some experience with investing, including higher risk assets such as equities and bonds. They can make up their minds on financial matters relatively quickly, but they still suffer some feelings of regret when their decisions turn out poorly. Mid-risk investors with time horizons of ten years or more typically have portfolios with a mix of higher-risk investments such as equities and lower-risk investments such as bonds and cash.

Mid-to-high-risk tolerance investors

With a risk tolerance in the mid-to-high range, investors are willing to take on investment risk and understand the nature of the long-term risk/return trade-off. They're willing to take risks with most of their available assets. Mid-to-high-risk investors are typically experienced investors who have used a range of investment products in the past. Mid-to-high-risk investors will usually be able to make up their minds on financial matters quickly. While they can suffer from regret when their decisions turn out poorly, they accept that occasional poor outcomes are a necessary part of long-term investment. Mid-to-high-risk investors with time horizons of ten years or more typically have portfolios that contain a majority of higher-risk investments such as equities but also bonds and cash.

High-risk tolerance investors

The high-risk tolerance investors want the highest possible return on their capital and are willing to take considerable amounts of risk to achieve this. They're usually willing to take risks with all of their available assets. High-risk investors typically have substantial amounts of investment experience. High-risk investors have firm investment views and will make up their minds on financial matters quickly. They do not suffer from regret to any great extent and can accept occasional poor outcomes easily. High-risk investors with time horizons of ten years or more typically have portfolios made up primarily of higher-risk investments such as equities, with little in bonds and cash.

Step Two:

Diversify Among the Three Main Asset Classes

Once you understand where you fall on the low-to-high risk spectrum and you have a good sense of the time horizon for each of your financial goals, you can work with your advisor to determine how to diversify your investments among the three main asset classes: stocks (equities), bonds (fixed-income), and cash (cash equivalents). Each class has a different level of risk and return, so each will behave differently over time.

> Most of my retirement is in the stock of the company I work for. I'm concerned.

Let's take a closer look at the characteristics of these three major asset classes:

Stocks (Equities): Highest risk/highest return

By owning a stock or stock fund you have an ownership interest in a company (or companies). As a shareholder, you benefit when the company does well and the stock price rises. If the company does not do well, the stock price may go down, causing the value of your shares to decline. Market, economic, financial, and political factors can all influence stock price. Investors who have long-term time horizons and are willing to weather volatile returns, e.g., those saving for retirement in twenty years, have generally been rewarded with strong positive returns.

Bonds (Fixed Income): Lower risk-return potential than stocks

Bonds are a loan to the US government, a state, or a company in which the organization receiving the loan repays investors with interest on the maturity date. The level of risk varies depending on the quality of the individual bond.

Overall, bonds are less volatile than stocks, but they offer more modest returns. As a result, an investor who is close to achieving a financial goal might increase bond holdings relative to stocks to lower risk.

The most productive way to get paid for taking risks is on the equity side of the portfolio (academic studies back this up). Therefore, use equity asset classes to take on risk and bonds to stabilize and reduce risk.

Cash (Cash Equivalents): Safest investment/lowest return
Cash and cash-equivalent investments include savings deposits, certificates of deposit (CDs), treasury bills, and money market deposit accounts. Because the federal government guarantees many of these investments, they are the safest asset class. Losses in non-guaranteed cash equivalents have been known to occur, but infrequently. Keep money safe and available in a cash-equivalent for a goal you are trying to achieve within three years.

Popular Investments to Avoid:
Let's look at three of them:

1. Gold
Gold is extremely volatile, which means when you add gold to your portfolio, you are taking on significant risk, and it's a risk that doesn't pay. This is because gold does not generate income

or earnings. Gold's only source of return is price appreciation caused by shifts in supply and demand. Therefore, unless you physically own gold coins or bars, it's best to stay away from this asset category.

> I bought all these gold coins in a panic when the stock market was down … and now they are worth a lot less than what I paid for them. I'm in a panic again.

Famed investor Warren Buffett summarized gold's low return potential in 2010 this way:

The world's gold stock is about 170,000 metric tons. If all of this gold were melded together, it would form a cube of about 68 feet per side. (Picture it fitting comfortably within a baseball infield.) At $1,750 per ounce—gold's price as I write this—its value would be $9.6 trillion. Call this cube pile A.

Let's now create a pile B costing an equal amount. For that, we could buy all US cropland (400 million acres with output of about $200 billion annually), plus 16 ExxonMobils (the world's most profitable company, one earning more than $40 billion annually). After these purchases, we would have about $1 trillion left over for walking-around money (no sense feeling strapped after this buying binge). Can you imagine an investor with $9.6 trillion selecting pile A over pile B?

2. Hedge Funds

Hedge funds are investment vehicles that make money by actively investing in a wide variety of asset classes. Unlike index funds, which invest in broad segments of the market and let the market do its work through patient investing, hedge fund managers are constantly trading, shorting, and using margins which lead to significantly higher fund fees—about 3.4 percent per year, versus the 0.15 – 0.35 percent per year charged by index funds. In addition to higher fees, hedge funds take an average 20 percent performance fee on any profits they generate. Hedge funds get away with this because they have limited transparency and light disclosure requirements.

Approximately 60 percent of all hedge funds tracked in the TASS Research Database have failed. Even those that have generated significant returns should be avoided, because once you take fees into account, the performance of hedge funds is generally lower than equity portfolios.

3. Real Estate Investment Trust

Real estate investment trusts (REITs) are often purchased for their income potential. REITs are companies that specialize in a segment of real estate such as office buildings, shopping centers, hospitals, or apartment complexes. An "index" REIT can add return and reduce risk. However, they are recommended only for tax-deferred or tax-free accounts such as IRAs and 401(k) accounts. This is because, by law, REITs are required to pay most of their income to investors, who then have to pay taxes on the income. Also, REIT dividends do not qualify for the same favorable tax treatment as corporate dividends.

Unfortunately, eight of the largest "nontraded" illiquid REITs barely broke even after seven years, assuming the dividends were reinvested. The sales commission to the broker is any-where from 7 to 15 percent, and many brokers mislead investors to use REITs as a bond substitute. Because of their expense and illiquidity, stay away from non-traded REITs.

4. Private Equity

Private-equity investments refer to ownership within companies. Ownership typically comes in the form of a limited partnership. Such investments are not traded or listed on public exchanges. Investments require a large sum of money by qualified investors and offer limited liquidity. As such, most investors don't meet the private-equity investment requirements.

Step Three:

Allocate Your Investments within the Three Major Classes

According to modern portfolio theory, only 6 percent of the overall gain experienced by the typical portfolio is related to picking the right stock. The lion's share of a portfolio's growth—up to 93 percent—comes from choosing the right mix of investments. Why? Because spreading your assets among many different investments decreases risk while it increases the potential gain.

For this reason, smart and patient investors use "asset allocation," i.e., they invest in a mix of assets within each of the three major asset classes. Because asset allocation aims to both preserve capital and grow wealth, it's considered a fail-safe principle of managing risk for an optimum return.

Start the process of allocating assets by working with your advisor to determine how much you want to invest in each of the three major asset classes. For example, depending upon your retirement objectives, you may choose to invest 60 percent in stocks, 35 percent in bonds, and 5 percent in cash equivalents (to cover short-term spending needs). Determining your asset allocation will be the most important decision you'll make about your investments—more important even than which specific investments you choose.

> Think of your investments as a group of pencils. While you could easily break a single pencil in half, when you put the pencils together in a group of four or five, they cannot be broken. Investments work the same way. A single asset class category can break under certain market conditions, but a properly diversified portfolio is exponentially stronger.

When choosing how to allocate your assets, focus on your portfolio's overall rate of return rather than the return within a specific asset class. At any given time, some asset classes may not perform as well as others. Don't get discouraged when this happens—a well-balanced portfolio is designed to withstand these ups and downs. The combination of investments determines your results.

A **conservative portfolio** includes mostly fixed-income investments, in which no more than 25 percent of assets are invested in equities.

A **moderate portfolio** is one in which between 30 percent and 60 percent of assets are invested in equities.

An **aggressive portfolio** is weighted toward equity investments, with at least 60 percent of assets invested in equity.

You and your advisor can determine the percentage you wish to allocate to each major class. Then further diversify your assets among investments within each asset class. Here are some asset class categories available in each asset class:

Equity Categories
- US Large
- US Large Value
- US Small
- US Small Value
- US Real Estate
- International Large
- International Large Value
- International Small
- International Small Value
- Emerging Markets

Bond Categories
- Short–Term US Government Bonds
- Short-Term Municipal Bonds

- Short-Term Investment Grade Bonds
- Short-Term Corporate Bonds
- Short-Term Global Bonds
- Inflation-Protected Bonds

Cash-equivalent Categories

- Savings accounts
- Certificates of deposit
- Treasury bills
- Money market funds

When is it appropriate to invest my cash in the market? I've been waiting, and it seems like I may have missed the big lift.

Step Four: Rebalance Your Portfolio

Once you've determined the appropriate asset allocation for your portfolio, devise a system for reviewing your goals and portfolio so that you can make sure your level of risk is in balance. This process is called rebalancing.

Rebalancing brings your portfolio back to your desired target allocation. This is necessary because over time some of your investments may become out of alignment with your investment goals—for example, when some investments grow faster than others. With rebalancing, you can make sure your portfolio does not overemphasize one or two asset class categories and maintains a comfortable level of risk.

Many factors can influence the overall balance of your portfolio, the predominant one being changes in the market. Let's say you designed a portfolio with 30 percent of assets invested in large-cap stocks. If the market for large caps does especially well one year, the overall amount of your portfolio invested in large caps might rise to 40 percent. At the same time, another asset class category, such as international stocks, could decrease. This would put the allocation of your portfolio out of balance based on your risk tolerance and capacity.

In order to rebalance your portfolio, you'd sell off a portion of large-cap stocks and reinvest the proceeds in international investments, devote any new contributions to underweighted asset class categories, or do both, until the portfolio is back in balance.

Regularly rebalancing your portfolio in this way brings *discipline* to the investment process. It takes reactiveness out of the equation and forces you to sell high and buy low—which is the opposite of what most reactive investors typically do.

Ideally, you should revisit your financial goals and assess the status of your portfolio at least once a year, or when the relative weight of an asset class increases or decreases more than a certain percentage identified in advance.

Questions to Ask Your Advisor

1. How do you help me determine my risk tolerance?

   Many advisors have assessments to help identify a client's tolerance for risk. Make sure your advisor's assessment takes into account behavioral (psychological) traits, the risk required to achieve your goals, and the capacity for risk calculated from your financial plan.

2. How do you decide my asset allocation?

   Your advisor should determine your asset allocation parameters based on your assessed level of risk.

3. How is my portfolio diversified?

   Your advisor should diversify your portfolio using sub-asset categories divided between equity and fixed-income investments.

4. How will you know my risk capacity?

   Risk capacity refers to the amount of risk you can afford to take based on your financial and life goals and expected revenue streams. If your advisor does not know your goals or revenue streams, they will have no ability to manage your risk capacity; therefore your portfolio may be at extreme risk in uncertain markets. A financial plan uncovers risk capacity.

5. During the Great Recession, how did you manage your
   clients' portfolios?

   *You want an advisor who took an active buy-and-hold
   strategy by rebalancing clients' accounts, had enough cash
   to capitalize on investment opportunities and handle
   distributions without taking a loss, and who revisited the
   financial plan to regain perspective and direction.*

6. When do you decide to sell an investment? Do you have an
   Investment Policy Statement (IPS)?

   *An IPS is a document that explains the firm's investment
   policies as well as the procedures the firm will follow while
   managing your investments. This statement typically outlines
   such things such as risk tolerance, investment objectives, types
   of investments, general portfolio allocations, investment time
   frames, and performance measures.*

CHAPTER 8

DISCIPLINED INVESTING WITH THE MULTIFACTOR MODEL

We have two classes of forecasters:
Those who don't know—and those who
don't know they don't know.

—JOHN KENNETH GALBRAITH,
Economist

If you were to chart the emotional cycle of the average investor, it might look something like this:

1. Hope - *I expect my investment to grow.*

2. Worry - *What if my investment doesn't grow?*

3. Relief - *Oh, thank God, my investment is growing.*

4. Worry - *Oh no … the value of my investment is dropping!*

5. Fear - *I'm losing money! What should I do?*

While the length of each phase varies, and the phases can arise in any order—fear can follow hope; worry can lead to more worry—the fact is that the majority of investors are stuck in an endless hope-worry cycle because they lack discipline.

Here's a money secret: the more disciplined you are with your investment strategy, the calmer you'll be. But being able to sleep at night—as welcome as that is—is only one advantage. The primary benefit of a disciplined approach to investing is that you'll be able to achieve your financial goals.

When I first started in financial services, I was with a brokerage firm whose primary objective was to sell—active mutual funds, annuities, and life insurance. When the markets were up, life was good. When the markets nose-dived, the clients got hurt. It was a wake-up call. I began to wonder:

> *What can an advisor do to create a more successful,*
> *less anxious investment experience for the client?*

Over the years, I've learned that you can't control markets, you can't control the behavior of other people related to the markets, and you certainly can't control what the financial media broadcasts about markets. I've also learned that you should not try to capitalize on the pricing "mistakes" of the market. Instead, I've discovered that the best way to help investors pursue higher returns is to focus on a portfolio's structure. How? By following a disciplined approach to investing.

So, what does a disciplined approach look like?

First, a disciplined approach is patient, long-term investing. It is the exact opposite of an active, let's-beat-the-market-now-with-

> I am naturally a skeptic, show me your data and prove to me your process and success.

this-hot-stock strategy. When you approach investing as a lifelong process, financial markets become your ally rather than your adversary. You can ride out market drops (which typically happen over the short term) and take advantage of market growth (which happens over the long term).

Second, a disciplined approach balances risk. Instead of avoiding risk (and losing the potential for financial gain) or taking on too much risk (and losing sleep), a disciplined approach balances risk and return in a structured way that captures the expected returns of each underlying asset class. Remember, it is impossible to have a high rate of return and no risk. To realize a higher rate of return, you have to take on some level of risk. However, you should not be taking risks that don't pay. Instead, you should be making investment decisions around the risk factors that carry the greatest potential for reward.

Third, a disciplined approach takes advantage of the multifactor model. The multifactor model, which is based upon decades of empirical academic research and is supported by Nobel Laureates, provides a framework for making investment decisions based on several factors of return.

Understanding the Relationship between Risk and Return

In any given year, low-risk treasury bills could outperform stocks. But historically, the investments that carry higher risk are the ones that produce significantly greater returns over time.

The chart below shows how a single dollar invested in four major asset classes would have grown between 1926 and 2014. It also illustrates how over the same time period, inflation would have changed the value of a dollar (in terms of price).

US Capital Market Returns
Growth of $1
January 1, 1926, to January 1, 2014

Source: Wealth Legacy Institute

Factor Investing: The holy grail of disciplined investment strategies

As discussed in Chapter 6, Debunking the Biggest Investment Myth, investing in index type funds that invest in a broad segment of the market is a discipline-driven first step to investing. There are, however, various *factors* that can be capitalized to provide market-beating returns without resorting to active investing. Combining factor investing with a tax-efficient, low-expense strategy often leads to better financial outcomes.

The Six Factors of Return

Multifactor investing is a strategy that incorporates six factors of return into a globally diversified portfolio.

Stock (Equities) Factors: Of the six factors of return, four will help you decide how to invest wisely in equities. These four factors are: 1) invest in the stock market; 2) invest in small companies; 3) purchase value over growth; and 4) invest based on the likelihood of higher profitability. Let's look at each of these factors in more detail.

1. The Market Factor: *Invest in stocks that have higher expected returns than bonds over time.*

Equities offer the potential for higher long-term investment returns than cash or fixed-income investments. Equities are also more volatile in their performance. Investors seeking higher rates of return must increase the proportion of equities in their portfolio while at the same time accepting greater variation of results. Caution: Don't speculate by purchasing individual stocks; own stock funds.

> I am taking a step, a baby step, but I am opening the door to go down this path.

Because markets are inherently efficient and have grown over time—something that is not true for individual stocks—you should own the whole market by investing in funds. Investing in funds is the foundation of the multifactor model, and every factor that follows is based on the purchase of collective funds, not single stocks.

2. The Company Size Factor: *Invest in small companies, that outperform large companies.*

Take a look at the graph on US Capital Market Returns. As you can see, small company stocks have consistently delivered higher returns than large company stocks. This is because small companies carry more risk. Yes, they have the ability to grow substantially, but they can also run out of money. Because of this higher risk, bankers charge higher lending rates to small startups than they do to large, established companies. They want to be paid for the increased risk of default.

Stock investors view risk the same way bankers do: because investing in smaller companies carries more risk, investors expect to be paid greater returns. Over time, investing in small company funds has proven to be a prudent investment strategy because small companies have the potential to grow more, in percentage terms, than larger established firms.

3. The Relative Price Factor: *Purchase value over growth.*

Purchase funds according to the value offered rather than the growth promised. To illustrate the principle of value-based investing, let's talk about cars.

Do you remember your first car? Was it new? Probably not, but it likely got you where you needed to go for relatively little money. This was certainly my experience. To get my first car, I paid $100 in parking violations for a friend, and she gave me her car in return. The car was not attractive, but dollar for dollar it got me farther than any car I've owned since. I like to think of that experience as little money in, many miles out.

"Little money in, many miles out" is also a great shorthand way to think about value-based investing. Value investments are not the glamorous stocks that lead the news. Instead, value funds generally consist of distressed or out-of-favor companies that are available at bargain prices. It's like comparing my first car to a new BMW. Dollar for dollar, value stocks have the potential to generate more mileage than the glitzy growth stocks.

4. The Expected Profitability Factor: *Invest based on higher expected profitability.*
Include firms in your portfolio with higher profitability relative to price, cash flow, or other metrics. Given two identical companies, the more profitable company will outperform the less profitable company. When all other factors are equal, the company that is more profitable must have a competitive advantage that drives its profits higher. Over time, these higher profits translate into higher expected returns. This is essentially the secret behind Warren Buffet's success.

Bond (Fixed-Income) Factors: The final two factors of return relate to investing in fixed-income funds such as municipal and treasury bonds. Because fixed-income investments carry less risk than stocks, they should be viewed as a stabilizer in your portfolio, a way to keep your money safe regardless of what is happening in the equity market. Here are the two fixed-income factors:

5. The Term Factor: *Buy bond funds with shorter time frames.*

Too many investors bring the equity market mindset to fixed-income investing; they try to make money by investing in bond funds that offer high yields over long periods of time. But longer-term bond funds carry higher risk and, unlike the stock market, it's typically not risk that pays.

Here's an example: say you invested $10,000 in a bond used to pay for the development of a new airport and the payoff date is twenty-five years from now. Although you would be paid interest annually, the long time frame locks up your money, preventing you from using it for other investments. If you bought the bond and it paid 5 percent interest, that interest rate would never rise—regardless of what else is happening in the markets. Interest rates could rise to 7 percent or 8 percent, and your money would be tied up in a bond paying less than the market rate for the next twenty-five years.

6. The Credit Quality Factor: *Buy high-quality bond funds.*

Bonds that have a low credit rating typically generate higher returns because they are riskier. But this increased risk also means the bond is more likely to default or be sold at a loss. Higher ratings, on the other hand, imply a lower risk, but the higher rating also means the interest rate will be lower. Because bonds are a stabilizer, you want to keep the risk low in your fixed-income portfolio. Do this by investing in bond funds with high-quality ratings. Standard and Poor's rating service measures and rates the credit risks of various bonds. Its ratings use the following grading system, expressed from highest to lowest:

AAA, AA, A, BBB, BB, B, CCC, CC, C. Anything below BBB
is considered non-investment grade or junk bonds.

Evaluating credit risk is like choosing tenants for a vacation
property. If it were legal, you could rent to a mature couple for $700
a week (high-quality investment grade), to the twenty-something
professional for $800 a week (low-quality investment-grade), or
to a group of college students for $1,000 a week (below investment
grade). As you can see, the potential profits increase with the
potential risks.

Market, Company Size, Relative Price, Expected Profitability

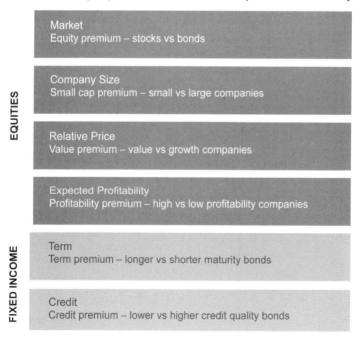

The Multifactor Model

How do you take advantage of the six factors of return? By using the *multifactor model* as one of your money secrets. Successful investing means not only targeting factors that generate higher expected return, but also managing risks that may needlessly compromise performance.

By allocating your portfolio among the six factors, your exposure to risk is calculated, balanced, disciplined and markets are allowed to work for you. The model is low cost and sensible, and it diversifies your investments across global markets and asset classes. Multifactor investing helps navigate tough market conditions by providing a repeatable framework to help your advisor make wise choices around diversification and asset allocation.

Spreading out your investments using the multifactor model is like creating meals using the food pyramid. Both ensure that you make balanced choices to create long-term health.

Patient Investing™ Comparing Passive, Factor and Active

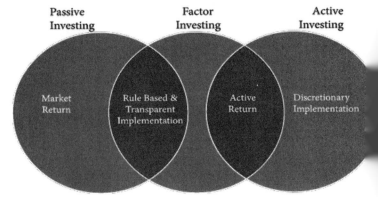

MSCI Research Insight, *Foundations of Factor Investing*. December 2013

Questions to Ask Your Advisor

1. What is your investment philosophy? Is there robust research to support his or her strategy?

   Look for a firm that creates portfolios using the multifactor model, in which stock choices represent the whole market and have a small-cap, value tilt that incorporates profitability. Look for a bond focus with short-term maturities and high credit quality. Does the strategy follow a process that is proven, documented, and repeatable? Is there a body of work or track record that connects the approach to actual results?

2. Do you believe in efficient markets?

   If the advisor does not believe in the efficient market hypothesis, he or she likely believes he or she has the capacity to beat the market through stock picking or forecasting. If that is the case— move on.

3. Do you have access to Dimensional Fund Advisors (DFA) asset class funds?

   If your advisor has access to Dimensional Fund Advisor funds, that is a significant plus, since DFA wrote the book on multifactor investing. Just make sure your potential advisor also does financial planning. DFA brings a scientific, empirical approach to investing, with advanced portfolio design, analysis, and investment discipline. DFA has some of the brightest minds on staff, including several Nobel Laureates in Economics. Its strategies are available to individual investors through a select group of independent, fee-only financial advisory firms.

(Disclosure: I routinely recommend DFA investments to clients and receive no compensation or kickbacks.)

4. In the Great Recession that peaked in March 2009, how many clients did you lose … and why?

   Your advisor's answer to this question will help you determine how well the advisor managed risk capacity, client communication, client emotions, and multifactor investing.

5. What is the average internal cost of the portfolio you would suggest for me?

   The advisor's internal portfolio cost—otherwise known as operating costs—should be below 0.50 percent, which is described as 50 basis points. A basis point is a unit that is equal to 1/100th of 1 percent. The relationship between percentage changes and basis points can be summarized as follows: 1 percent change = 100 basis points and 0.01 percent = 1 basis point.

   For example, for a $500,000 portfolio, the average internal investment cost might be 35 basis points—or 0.35 percent. This means the internal operating costs associated with managing that portfolio would be $1,750 annually.

CHAPTER 9

PAIN-FREE STEPS TO FIRE YOUR ADVISOR

Every new beginning comes from
some other beginning's end.

—SENECA

When I consider what tremendous consequences
come from little things … I am tempted to think
there are no little things.

—BRUCE BARTON

I f, after reading this book, you have the nagging feeling that your current financial advisor may not be right for you, trust that feeling. You've worked hard to save your money over the years and have made several trade-offs in the process. No matter what your personal feelings may be for your current advisor, if you no longer believe the advisor has your best long-term financial interests in mind, fire that person.

This is not only your money we're talking about, this is your life. The longer you maintain an unsatisfying financial relationship, the more it will cost you.

If your gut is telling you to move on, and if your head is telling you the results you've seen have been unsatisfactory, you are not alone. An estimated 25 percent of investors are unhappy with their current financial advisor, with women and high-net-worth investors being the most dissatisfied. Ironically, women typically stay in a mediocre advisory relationship far longer than men do.

If you're the type of person who likes to gather concrete evidence (in support of your intuition) before making a decision, here are some indicators that it's time to fire your current advisor and find a fee-only financial fiduciary:

- **Your current advisor is a salesperson.** You've learned from reading this book and asking the right questions that your advisor receives commissions and kickbacks on the investments they make on your behalf.

- **Your current advisor actively chases returns.** Your advisor makes frequent trades and changes course often with no clear investment objective. This makes them an active investor who foolishly chases "hot" stocks or mutual funds and tries to beat the market—at your expense.

- **Your current advisor offers bad advice.** He has put you into mutual funds or alternative investments with expensive management fees and sales charges, or encouraged you to buy expensive products such as annuities or hedge funds.

Your advisor pretends to know the "perfect" time to invest. There's no such thing as "perfect" in the investment world.

- **Your current advisor is unable to explain basic concepts** or to answer the questions at the end of each chapter in this book.

- **Your current advisor does not communicate**. The advisor doesn't call or email regularly and doesn't return calls promptly.

- **Your current advisor does not listen to your questions, talks down to you**, and does not understand your specific financial needs. (Fact: This is the number one reason women fire their advisor after the death or divorce of a spouse.)

- **Your current advisor has not created a comprehensive financial plan for you.** Without a plan, how will you or your advisor know if you are on track to reach your goals?

- **You feel no chemistry with your current advisor**. There is a lack of personal touch, and there are no personal or professional interests that connect you. Without chemistry, it is difficult to have trust.

Ending the Relationship

Okay, you've decided it's over. Let's assume that now you're ready to move ahead. Ending any kind of relationship is never easy. It can feel antagonistic and stimulate feelings of betrayal, anger, confusion, and other emotions we all wish to avoid.

This is especially true when you like your financial advisor, or when your advisor is a member of the family or a personal friend. What's important to know is that the financial industry relies on brokers signing up friends and family members as clients. These are the people who will most likely give their trust to a new broker. But liking someone is not a good enough reason to put your entire portfolio—and future—at risk.

Once you've decided to end the relationship, transferring your accounts is easier than you think. You have only one thing to do to transfer your accounts.

That *one thing* is to find the right financial fiduciary for you and your family, using the guidelines in this book. As a reminder, your new advisor should:

1. Be a fee-only financial fiduciary who charges a basic investment management fee to manage your portfolio. He or she receives no hidden fees, kickbacks, fee-sharing, rebates, or commissions.

2. Do comprehensive financial planning integrated with your investment portfolio and your new advisor should charge a separate financial planning fee because it is a separate process.

3. Understand and take into account your emotions and values around money, instead of jumping right into action and investing.

4. Be a Certified Financial Planner® who proudly prints the letters CFP after his or her name.

Transferring Your Accounts

Once you've found the right fee-only financial fiduciary, the funds transfer process is relatively painless and can be completed in three easy steps.

Step 1 *Provide your new advisor with a recent statement of all the accounts you wish to transfer.* These statements will provide your new advisor with individual account numbers so that they can track each transfer from your old advisor to your new advisor's custodian, the third-party repository that keeps your money safe and ensures that your advisor has no ability to pocket it.

Step 2 *Decide how you wish to transfer your assets.* Do you wish to convert all your investments to cash (through liquidation) or do you wish to transfer your investments exactly as they are (an "in-kind" transfer)? There are pros and cons to both approaches. Talk with your new advisor to determine what is best for your situation.

Be aware that there may be some surrender fees involved in the transfer process. You may have a transfer fee imposed for closing out accounts, for example. On average, the surrender fee for brokerage firms ranges from $75 to $100 per account. Some mutual funds also have surrender charges, depending on the share class. You may also owe some fees, depending on the agreement with your current advisor, such as trade fees on assets that need to be sold before transfer.

Investors cannot escape most fees, but your new financial fiduciary should be able to save a great deal in costs the first year alone through Patient Investing, which can make these fees look miniscule by comparison.

Step 3 *Once you've decided what assets to transfer and how, your new advisor will initiate the transfer process.* You only need to sign paperwork. (This can be done in person, by mail, or through electronic signature.) It's that simple. This paperwork initiates the transfer of your money from your old advisor to your new one.

The movement of money is usually done electronically or through the Automated Customer Account Transfer System (ACATS), a standardized system that financial firms use to move client accounts from one firm to another. Your new advisor will monitor the transfer process and make sure it proceeds seamlessly.

You do not need to talk with your current advisor or tell him or her anything at this point. In fact, if you're certain of your desire to end the relationship, transfer your funds before talking to the current advisor. Otherwise, he/she may try to talk you into staying. If that happens, simply say, "No thank you. I've made up my mind."

After the assets have been transferred, you may then decide if you wish to contact your old advisor and share your reasons for leaving. For most advisors, a client breakup is not dramatic.

Financial Advisor Selection Flow Chart

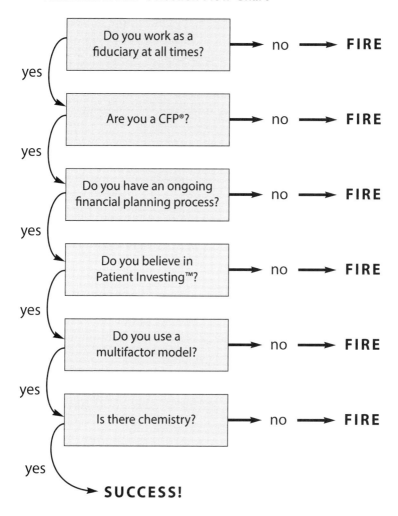

Smart advisors view breakups as a regular course of business and may ask what they could have done differently to keep your business. Be honest. There's no reason not to be.

If you are firing a friend or family member, you may wish to alert him or her to the end of the relationship by saying, "I value our personal relationship so much that I didn't want money to affect us, so I've decided to move it elsewhere."

It usually takes two to three weeks once paperwork has been submitted for assets to show up at your new advisor's custodian. No trades or distributions—including ongoing IRA contributions or systematic monthly distributions—should be made until the transfer is complete.

Once the transfer is complete, you can begin working with your new advisor to create the financial security and life you've long envisioned.

Follow the questions in the flow chart, moving downwards when evaluating your current advisor or selecting a new, fee-only financial fiduciary. If the answer to any question is "no," move on until you find an advisor who can answer every question with a confident and assertive "yes!"

CHAPTER 10

FINAL THOUGHTS

The need for change bulldozed a road
down the center of my mind.

—MAYA ANGELOU

Now that you've reached the end of *Money Secrets,* hopefully you've gotten a good start on creating an integrated financial planning and investment portfolio, as well as a more confident and relaxed approach to life. My sincere hope is that *Money Secrets* has opened the door for you to:

- Understand your own emotional relationship with money;

- Understand the principles of solid investing;

- Realize how vitally important financial planning is to your future;

- Know how to hire a fee-only financial fiduciary that has your best interests in mind; and

- Ask questions of a new or existing advisor to discern whether or not the advisor is a good fit.

In short, you've now gained the knowledge and tools to get the right plans and people in place.

I know, from working with countless clients for the last twenty years, that when you succeed in investing, your confidence and self-worth will flourish. Plus, you will inspire others, including your spouse, children, grandchildren, and friends, to follow in your footsteps. Your financial confidence will empower them to create their own financial strength and well-being. Now, that's what I call leaving a legacy!

I wish you the best of luck on your new financial journey!

—Kim

ABOUT THE AUTHOR

Kim Curtis, CFP®, ChFC®, CLU®, CAP®, AEP®, MSFS, is the President and CEO of Wealth Legacy Institute. She is a nationally recognized wealth management advisor and speaker. Her groundbreaking work in developing Humanigraphix,™ a highly personal client-centric legacy planning model, was recognized in the *Journal of Practical Estate Planning,* winning the Editor's Choice award.

The *Planning for LIFE Experience™* is the cornerstone of her firm's holistic and highly successful approach to integrated wealth management.

Kim has been profiled in several publications including the *Wall Street Journal.* She has attained numerous professional designations and been recognized by the financial planning industry as having achieved the highest level of competence and expertise in comprehensive financial planning. Additionally, her education includes an MSJA from the University of Denver's Sturm College of Law, an MSFS from the American College in finance, and a B.S. from Elmira College in judicial administration.

Kim Curtis lives in Denver, Colorado, with her family.

WORKING WITH KIM

Connect with Kim Curtis for Speaking at your conference or for your organization at: **KimCurtisSpeaker.com**

To follow the Blogs or Investing and Financial Planning, follow Wealth Legacy Institute at:

WealthLegacyInstitute.com/blog

 @KimCurtisLegacy

 Facebook.com/WealthLegacyInstitute

 LinkedIn.com/KimberlyCurtis

 Pinterest.com/WLILegacy

 YouTube.com/WLILegacy

WEALTH LEGACY
INSTITUTE

Wealth Legacy Institute is an independent wealth management firm that helps individuals and families gain financial confidence and security. Its mission is to serve as a beacon for financial freedom and family sustainability.

The firm was founded on the philosophy that long-term, collaborative, fiduciary relationships with clients are essential to ultimate family financial success. By having an independent, fee-only professional who acts as a fiduciary (similar to a CPA or an attorney), clients receive unbiased advice that is in their best interest, unconstrained by the inherent conflicts that arise when a registered representative stands in as a financial advisor.

Wealth Legacy Institute's proprietary *Planning for LIFE Experience*™ helps transform the LIFE clients' dreams, into the LIFE they experience. *Patient Investing*™ is the cornerstone of Wealth Legacy Institute's investment philosophy that is fundamental to better financial outcomes.

WealthLegacyInstitute.com

Want to learn more about yourself and your money? Take the comprehensive, free online communications assessment at *WealthLegacyInstitute.com.*

Interested in regular updates on the art and science of money? Subscribe to *Behind the Money,* a free quarterly email newsletter at *WealthLegacyInstitute.com*

For a list of the documents you will likely need to gather to begin the financial planning process, go to *WealthLegacyInstitute.com* and download *Document Checklist*.

Acknowledgements

This book represents many years of accumulated knowledge, experience and input from clients, friends and colleagues. I am grateful for all these enriching associations in my life.

MY CLIENTS: thank you, thank you and thank you! The best part of my work is witnessing how you have made your dream life a reality. Thank you for sharing your stories and trusting our work. Your gratitude has made the journey extremely rewarding. You are the people who inspire me daily and who convinced me to write this book.

SHARI CAUDRON AND THE NARRATIVE GROUP: Your professionalism and commitment to this project over the years has been encouraging. Thank you for helping me become a better writer.

THE BOOK SHEPHERD: Dr. Judith Briles and her team with Rebecca Finkel guided this book to completion. That was an undertaking.

CONTRIBUTORS: Robin Colucci, Lucia Brown, Nick Zelinger, Kathi and Hobie Dunn, Melanie Smithson and NSA Colorado members for sharing your expertise and insights.

TEAM WEALTH LEGACY INSTITUTE: I am honored to be working with such talented individuals. Your innovation, stewardship, advocacy, passion for excellence and creativity in providing services and tools to help our clients succeed is why we love our work. Niels Jepsen, Shannon Johnson, Susan Saunders and Meg Gehl—thank you all!

COUNT ME IN FOR WOMEN'S ECONOMIC INDEPENDENCE: an entrepreneur community that gave me tools, resources and a peer exchange platform: Nell Merlino, Isisara Bey, Alicia Marie at People Biz and BAM gals Michele Conklin, Wendy Phillips, Charlene Meriwether and Simla Somturk for all your insight and encouragement.

MY FAMILY: Meg, Arden and Hunter who continually challenge my assumptions and keep me open to new possibilities.

I am grateful to all of you from the bottom of my heart.

APPENDIX

3 Steps to Creating your Humanigraphix™
Step 1. Mapping Family Structure

The basic symbols to construct a humanigraphix are illustrated below:

Symbol	Label	Symbol	Label
○	Female	□⫻○	Divorce
□	Male	□╱○	Separation
□——○	Married	□┬○ ○	Adopted
□····○	Unmarried Relationship		
□〰○	Hostile	□╱\○ □ □	Twins
□══○	Close		
□-‖-○	Cut off	⊠	Death

Males are drawn to the left of females when married and children are drawn in birth order with the oldest to youngest being drawn from left to right.

Step 2. Documenting Family Information

Once the family structure has been drawn, the next step is to include information about the family such as demographics, functional information and critical family events. Demographics may include date of birth, age, date of death, occupation or educational level. Functional information is about the overall health and well-being of your different family members, such as alcohol or drug addictions, obesity, gambling, diabetes, over-spending or depression. Critical family events include important transitions, such as marriages, divorces, moves or job changes. These may be written in the margins of your graph or use a separate paper documenting the family chronology.

Here are some questions that may be helpful in capturing your family information:

- What do you see as the strengths and weaknesses of your family?
- What are the core values of your family?
- How are those values expressed?
- How are financial decisions made in your family?
- Who controls the money? Who makes the spending decisions? Investment decisions? Are these patterns different from the way money was handled in your family of origin?
- How does your economic situation compare with your relatives? Why the difference?
- Is there any expected inheritance? Are there family members you support or will need to care for in the future?

Step 3. Delineating Family Relationships

This last step understands the relationships between your family members. The following questions can help capture details about your family relationships:

- Are there family members who do not speak to each other or have ever had a period of not speaking?
- Are the relationships cooperative, competitive or contentious?
- What are some of the family rules, norms or understandings about behavior?
- What is the family's work ethic? Are there generational differences?
- What are your culture's values regarding male and female roles? Education? Family connectedness? Family caretaking? Religious practices? Have these values changed over time?
- Who helps out when help is needed?
- Are sensitive issues openly discussed?
- How does each parent get along with each child? What are the power dynamics in the family? Are certain family members intimidated by others? Do some family members have more power to define what will happen in relationships?
- Has any family member been characterized as a problem one? Caretaker? Sick one? Bad one? Successful? Failure?
- Who is seen as warm, cold, caring or distant?
- For you individually, the vertical axis includes your biological heritage and other aspects of your genetic makeup. These factors can manifest physically and emotionally. The horizontal axis relates to your development over your lifespan. This can be influenced by your relationships, migration, health and success.

At the family level, the vertical axis includes all the family attitudes, taboos, expectations, labels and loaded issues that family members learn as they grow. The horizontal flow at the family level describes the family as it moves through time, coping and transitioning through death, birth, job loss and chronic illness.

Scanning the breadth of your family helps understand the family's strengths and struggles in relation to money and legacy planning. When you look at the present with regards to themes, myths, rules, and emotionally charged issues of previous generations, repetitive patterns often become clear.

You can begin to put behaviors into context, which may help in appreciating your history and your legacy. Humanigraphix may help neutralize attitudes surrounding negative behaviors such as "Grandpa's tight with money," which may be seen as a result of being raised during the Depression era.

When creating a humanigraphix, the goal is to feel more connected to your intersection between money and life. You recognize connections between your own distresses and desires, past and present, and those connections promote a sense of hope for your future.

The Financial Advisor Fiduciary Oath

THIS FIDUCIARY OATH is made and entered into, effective _____, by and between _____("Client") and _____("Financial Advisor").

The Financial Advisor shall always act in good faith and in the best interests of the Client(s) as their fee-only financial fiduciary in every transaction and in every situation.

The Financial Advisor shall provide written disclosure to the Client prior to the engagement, and throughout the term of the engagement, of any conflicts of interest that will or reasonably might be considered to compromise the impartiality or independence of the Financial Advisor.

The Financial Advisor, or any party or firm in whom the Financial Advisor has a financial interest, does not receive any compensation or other remuneration that is contingent on any Client's purchase or sale of a financial product.

The Financial Advisor does not receive a fee or other compensation from another party based on the referral of a Client or the Client's business.

The Financial Advisor does not receive any marketing incentives from any mutual fund company or firm to assist in business growth.

Signed this _____ of _____

_____
Financial Advisor

_____
Client(s)

_____

_____

What is Your Financial Planning Philosophy?

1. What is important to you? What matters most in life? Is it your family? Contributing to others? Remaining healthy and active? Continuing to learn and grow? Think about your priorities in life, not only from a financial standpoint, but also physically (your health), emotionally (how you want to feel about your life), and socially (how you want to give to others).

2. In the next three to five years, what has to happen for you to feel happy about your progress? You might start by thinking about your financial picture, but also consider your family, health, career, and spiritual growth. There are no wrong answers here. One person might be focused on selling his business at a profit, another might want to spend a year after retirement dedicating her expertise to a nonprofit, and someone else might be focused on getting into shape and running a marathon.

3. How do you plan to realize your life's potential? Do you want to spend more time volunteering as a storyteller at the local library? Do you want to go back to school for a master's in education? Have you wanted to write a novel?

4. What are the best and worst decisions you have made in any area of your life? Have you made financial mistakes? Experienced career highs? Made brilliant choices when it came to children and where to live? Think about your particular successes and failures.

5. What do you want to have more of in life? Time? Money? Vacations? Family? What are you passionate about? Where would you like to focus more of your attention?

6. How do you typically make financial decisions? Do you conduct a lot of research? Discuss investments with your spouse? Read financial magazines or websites? Follow the suggestions of neighbors? How—and when—have you gotten off track with your finances?

7. If you did not wake up tomorrow, what would you most regret not having done? Is your potential regret related to your family, your health, or your particular talents? What might you need to do now to start achieving this goal?

What Do All Those Letters Mean?
CFP®—Certified Financial Planner

- Requirements: Bachelor's degree, education requirements, and three years of experience.
- Exam: Comprehensive ten-hour exam.
- CFP and Certified Financial Planner marks are certification marks owned by the Certified Financial Planner Board of Standards, Inc. These marks are awarded to individuals who successfully complete the CFP Board's initial and ongoing certification requirements.
- Those wanting to become a CFP professional must take extensive exams in the areas of financial planning, taxes, insurance, estate planning, and retirement. Attaining the CFP designation takes experience and a substantial amount of work. CFP professionals must also complete continuing-education programs each year to maintain their certification status.
- Certified Financial Planners agree to a strict code of professional conduct and ethics. This code of ethics and financial responsibility comprises seven principles: integrity, objectivity, competence, fairness, confidentiality, professionalism, and diligence. Certified Financial Planners who violate these principles are subject to disciplinary action, that can include the loss of the license.

ChFC®—Chartered Financial Consultant

- Requirements: three years of experience and completion of seven required courses and the selection of two electives:

- Financial Planning: Process & Environment
- Fundamentals of Insurance Planning
- Income Taxation
- Planning for Retirement Needs
- Investments
- Fundamentals of Estate Planning
- Financial Planning Applications
- Select two electives: Financial System & Economy, Estate Planning for Executives, Executive Compensation, Financial Decisions for Retirement
- Exam: At end of each course.
- The designation has been a mark of excellence for financial planners for almost thirty years and currently requires more courses than any other financial planning credential. The curriculum covers extensive education and application training in all aspects of financial planning, income taxation, investments, and estate and retirement planning.
- Chartered Financial Consultants must adhere to The American College of Financial Services' Code of Ethics, which includes the following professional pledge: "I shall, in light of all conditions surrounding those I serve, which I shall make every conscientious effort to ascertain and understand, render and service which, in the same circumstances, I would apply to myself."
- Designation may be removed for unethical conduct through the certification committee of The American Colleges Board of Trustees.

CLU®—Chartered Life Underwriter

- Requirements: Three years of experience and completion of eight courses.
- Exam: after each course
- CLU is one of the oldest and most respected credentials in financial services, dating back to the late 1920s. It represents a thorough understanding of a broad array of personal risk management and life insurance planning issues and stresses ethics, professionalism, and in-depth knowledge in the delivery of financial advice.
- Chartered Life Underwriters must adhere to The American College's Code of Ethics, which includes the following professional pledge: "I shall, in light of all conditions surrounding those I serve, which I shall make every conscientious effort to ascertain and understand, render that service which, in the same circumstances, I would apply to myself."
- Designation may be removed for unethical conduct through the certification committee of The American College's Board of Trustees.

CAP®—Chartered Advisor in Philanthropy

- Requirements: Three years of experience and three graduate-level courses.
- Exam: Three two-hour proctored exams.
- The advisor earning the CAP designation has taken three courses in philanthropy covering various impacts of planning for family wealth, charitable giving, and gift planning for nonprofits. The courses are offered through the Irwin Graduate School of The American College.

- Every two years, a CAP must complete 15 hours of continuing education in coursework directly related to the material required to obtain the CAP designation.
- Designation may be removed for unethical conduct through the certification committee of The American College's board of trustees.

AEP®—Accredited Estate Planner

- Requirements: a JD, CPA, CLU, ChFC, CFP, or CTFA certification. Five years of experience and two graduate-level courses.
- The AEP credential recognizes graduate-level specialization in estate planning, obtained in addition to already recognized professional credentials within the various disciplines of estate planning. It's awarded to estate planning professionals who meet stringent requirements of experience, knowledge, education, professional reputation, and character.
- The National Association of Estate Planners & Counselors (NAEPC) Code of Ethics is intended to align with those of the gateway professional designations required prior to earning the AEP.
- Every twenty-four months, an AEP must complete thirty hours of continuing education, including 15 hours in estate planning. Recertification is required annually.

MSFS—Masters of Science in Financial Services

- A master's degree for financial services professionals whose goal in client services is to maintain the highest level of technical knowledge and practical application in serving their clients.

- The MSFS is designed to allow professionals to keep current in a particular area or to pursue knowledge encompassing all aspects of financial planning. Financial services professionals who attain the MSFS degree will have the best preparation for practice in the financial planning profession.

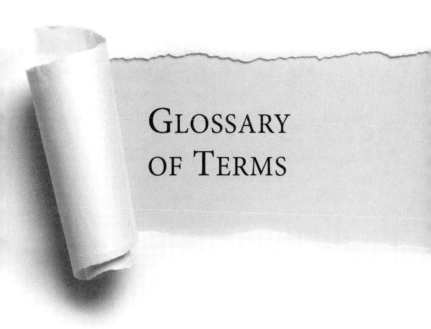

GLOSSARY OF TERMS

401(k) Plan: A qualified plan established by an employer, to which eligible employees may make salary deferral (salary reduction) contributions on a post-tax basis, pre-tax-basis, or both. Employers offering a 401(k) plan may make matching or non-elective contributions to the plan on behalf of eligible employees and may also add a profit sharing feature to the plan. Earnings accrue on a tax-deferred basis.

Active Investing: The use of a human element, such as a single manager, co-managers or a team of managers, to actively manage a fund's portfolio. Active managers rely on analytical research, forecasts, and their own judgment and experience in making investment decisions on what securities to buy, hold, and sell. The opposite of active management is called passive management, better known as "indexing."

Alpha: Measures the difference between a fund portfolio's actual return and its expected performance, given its beta and the actual returns of the benchmark index. Alpha is often seen as a measurement of the value added or subtracted by a portfolio's manager.

Asset Allocation: An investment strategy that aims to balance risk and reward by apportioning a portfolio's assets according to an individual's goals, risk tolerance, and time horizon.

Asset Class: A group of securities that exhibit similar characteristics, behave similarly in the marketplace, and are subject to the same laws and regulations. The three main asset classes are equities (stocks), fixed-income securities (bonds), and cash equivalents (money market instruments).

Beta: A measure of the degree of change in value one can expect in a portfolio given a change in value in a benchmark index, e.g., S&P 500. A portfolio with a beta of less than one is generally less volatile than its benchmark index.

Bond: A debt investment in which an investor loans money to an entity (corporate or governmental) for a defined period of time at a fixed interest rate. Bonds are used by companies, municipalities, states, and national governments to finance a variety of projects and activities. Bonds are commonly referred to as fixed-income securities and are one of the three main asset classes, along with stocks and cash equivalents.

Broker/Broker-Dealer: A person or firm in the business of buying and selling securities that operates as both a broker and a dealer, depending on the transaction. The term broker-dealer is used in US securities regulation parlance to describe stock brokerages, because most of them act as both agents and principals. A brokerage acts as a broker (or agent) when it executes orders on behalf of clients, whereas it acts as a dealer (or principal) when it trades for its own account.

Capital Gains: The profit from selling a capital asset at a higher price than you purchased it for.

Certificate of Deposit (CD): A savings certificate entitling the bearer to receive interest. A CD bears a maturity date, has a specified fixed interest rate, and can be issued in any denomination.

CDs are generally issued by commercial banks and are insured by the FDIC. The term of a CD generally ranges from one month to five years.

Commodity: (1.) A basic good used in commerce that is interchangeable with other commodities of the same type. Commodities are most often used as inputs in the production of other goods or services. The quality of a given commodity may differ slightly, but it is essentially uniform across producers. When they are traded on an exchange, commodities must also meet specified minimum standards, also known as a basis grade. (2.) Any good exchanged during commerce, which includes goods traded on a commodity exchange.

Credit Risk: The risk of loss of principal or loss of a financial reward stemming from a borrower's failure to repay a loan or otherwise meet a contractual obligation. Credit risk arises whenever a borrower is expecting to use future cash flows to pay a current debt. Investors are compensated for assuming credit risk by way of interest payments from the borrower or issuer of a debt obligation. Credit risk is closely tied to the potential return of an investment, the most notable being that the yields on bonds correlate strongly to their perceived credit risk.

Diversification: A risk management technique that mixes a wide variety of investments within a portfolio. The rationale behind this technique contends that a portfolio of different kinds of investments will, on average, yield higher returns and pose a lower risk than any individual investment found within the portfolio.

Dividend: A distribution of a portion of a company's earnings, decided by the board of directors, to a class of its shareholders. The dividend is most often quoted in terms of the dollar amount each share receives (dividends per share). It can also be quoted in terms of a percentage of the current market price, referred to as dividend yield.

Equity: A stock or any other security representing an ownership interest. The term's meaning depends very much on the context. In finance, in general, you can think of equity as ownership in any asset after all debts associated with that asset are paid off. For example, a car or house with no outstanding debt is considered the owner's equity because he or she can readily sell the item for cash. Stocks are equity because they represent ownership in a company.

Fiduciary: The person who looks after assets on another's behalf is legally responsible to act in the best interests of the person whose assets they are in charge of. This is known as "fiduciary duty."

Financial Advisor: A professional who helps individuals manage their finances by providing advice on money issues such as investments, insurance, mortgages, college savings, estate planning, taxes, and retirement depending on what the client requests. Some financial advisors are paid a flat fee for their advice, while others earn commissions from the investments they sell to their clients. Fee-only arrangements are widely regarded to be better for the client.

Financial Plan: A comprehensive evaluation of an investor's current and future financial state that uses currently known variables to predict future cash flows, asset values, and withdrawal plans. Most individuals work in conjunction with an investment or tax professional to develop a financial plan, using current net worth, tax liabilities, asset allocation, and future retirement and estate plans, along with estimates of asset growth, to determine if a person's financial goals can be met in the future.

Fund Category: A way of differentiating mutual funds according to their investment objectives and principal investment features. This categorization allows investors to spread their money around in a mix of funds with a variety of risk and return characteristics.

Humanigraphix™: An organized pictorial illustration that plots family membership and structure. It's an orienting map of the family history, patterns, relationships and values. These patterns across generations provide insight on family transitions and financial motivations. The advisor better understand a client's historical strengths and struggles in developing an integrated wealth plan.

Index: A type of mutual fund with a portfolio constructed to match or track the components of a market index, such as the Standard & Poor's 500 Index (S&P 500). An index mutual fund is said to provide broad market exposure, low operating expenses, and low portfolio turnover. Investing in an index fund is a form of passive investing. The primary advantage to such a strategy is the lower management expense ratio on an index fund. Also, a majority of mutual funds fail to beat broad indexes, such as the S&P 500.

Inflation: The rate at which the general level of prices for goods and services is rising, and, consequently, purchasing power is falling. Central banks attempt to prevent severe inflation, as well as severe deflation, to keep the excessive growth of prices to a minimum.

Inflation Risk: The risk that prices for goods and services will rise, shrinking purchasing power. As inflation rises, every dollar will buy a smaller percentage of a good. For example, if the inflation rate is 2 percent, then a $1 pack of gum will cost $1.02 in a year.

Interest Rate: The amount charged, expressed as a percentage of principal, by a lender to a borrower for the use of assets. Interest rates are typically noted on an annual basis, known as the annual percentage rate (APR). The assets borrowed could include cash, consumer goods, and large assets such as a vehicle or building. Interest is essentially a rental, or leasing, charged to the borrower, for the asset's use. In the case of a large asset, like a vehicle or building, the interest rate is sometimes known as the "lease rate." Low-risk borrowers will usually be charged a low interest rate. If the borrower is considered high risk, the interest rate will be higher.

Interest Rate Risk: The risk that the value of a fixed-income will change because of a change in the absolute level of interest rates, in the spread between two rates, in the shape of the yield curve, or in any other interest rate relationship. Such changes usually inversely affect securities and can be reduced by diversifying (investing in fixed-income securities with different durations) or hedging, e.g., through an interest rate swap.

Load: A sales charge or commission charged to an investor who buys or redeems shares in a mutual fund. The fee may be a one-time charge levied either when the investor buys into the mutual fund (front-end load) or when the investor redeems the mutual fund shares (back-end load).

Market Cycle: Trends or patterns that may exist in a given market environment, allowing some securities or asset classes to outperform others. The securities themselves may exhibit price patterns in their trading.

Market Risk: The possibility that an investor will experience losses due to factors that affect the overall performance of the financial markets. Market risk, also called "systematic risk," cannot be eliminated through diversification. The risk that a major natural disaster will cause a decline in the market as a whole is an example of market risk. Other sources of market risk include recessions, political turmoil, changes in interest rates, and terrorist attacks.

Market Timing: The act of attempting to predict the future direction of the market, typically through the use of technical indicators or economic data.

Maturity: A finite period of time during which a financial instrument remains outstanding. At the end of this period, the financial instrument will cease to exist and the principal will be repaid with interest. The term is most commonly used in the context of fixed-income investments such as bonds and deposits.

Modern Portfolio Theory (MPT): A theory of how rational investors construct portfolios to maximize expected return based on a given level of risk, emphasizing that risk is an inherent part of higher reward. There are four basic steps involved in portfolio construction: (1) security valuation, (2) asset allocation, (3) portfolio optimization, and (4) performance measurement.

Multifactor Investing: The multifactor model is based upon decades of empirical research supported by Nobel Laureates that provides a framework for making investment decisions based on six factors of return: Market, Company Size, Relative Price, Expected Profitability, Term and Credit Quality. The model does this by diversifying investments across global markets and asset classes.

Multifactor Model: A financial model that employs multiple factors in its computations to explain market phenomena, equilibrium asset prices, or both. A multifactor model can explain either an individual security or a portfolio of securities. It will do this by comparing two or more factors to analyze relationships between variables and the security's resulting performance.

Passive Investing: A style of management associated with mutual and exchange-traded funds (ETFs) in which a fund's portfolio mirrors a market index. Passive management is the opposite of active management, in which a fund's managers attempt to beat the market with various investing strategies and buying/selling decisions. It is also known as "passive strategy," or "index investing."

Patient Investing™: An investment philosophy that strives to outperform the market over the long-term by structuring portfolios along factors of expected return. The strategy is based on quantitative academic research, portfolio structure and avoiding behavioral biases. Proponents are Nobel Laureates Eugene Fama and Ken French.

Planning for LIFE Experience™: Wealth Legacy Institute's proprietary integrated wealth management process involving four stages: Discover, Design, Make Good and Grow. The process integrates a human behavioral approach with a tactical quantitative structure. This helps clients navigate tough market conditions by providing a repeatable framework to measure success and allow life to be at the center of the integrated wealth plan.

Qualified Retirement Plan: A plan that meets Internal Revenue Code requirements and, as a result, is eligible to receive certain tax benefits. These plans must be for the exclusive benefit of employees or their beneficiaries.

Rebalancing: The process of realigning the weighted percentages of portfolio asset classes. Rebalancing involves periodically buying or selling assets in your portfolio to maintain your original desired level of asset allocation.

Registered Representative (RR): A person who works for a brokerage company that is licensed by the Securities and Exchange Commission (SEC) and acts as an account executive for clients trading investment products such as stocks, bonds, and mutual funds.

Risk Tolerance: The degree of change in investment returns that an individual is willing to withstand. Risk tolerance is an important component in investing. An individual should have a realistic understanding of his or her ability and willingness to stomach large swings in the value of his or her investments. Investors who take on too much risk may panic and sell at the wrong time.

Security: A financial instrument that represents an ownership position in a publicly-traded corporation (stock), a creditor relationship with governmental body or a corporation (bond), or rights to ownership as represented by an option. A security is a fungible, negotiable financial instrument that represents some type of financial value. The company or entity that issues the security is known as the issuer.

Shareholder: Any person, company, or institution that owns at least one share of a company's stock. Shareholders are the company's owners. They have the potential to profit if the company does well, but that comes with the potential to lose if the company does poorly. A shareholder may also be referred to as a "stockholder."

Sharpe Ratio: Uses a portfolio's standard deviation and total return to determine reward per unit of risk. The higher the number in the ratio, the more return per unit of risk taken.

Standard Deviation: A statistical measure of the volatility of a portfolio's returns around its mean. The mean generally is a market index, e.g., S&P 500, that consists of holdings in the same asset class.

Time Horizon: The length of time over which an investment is made or held before it is liquidated. Time horizons can range from seconds, in the case of a day trader, all the way up to decades for a buy-and-hold investor.

Treasury Bill (T-Bill): A short-term debt obligation backed by the US government with a maturity of less than one year. T-bills are sold in denominations of $1,000 up to a maximum purchase of $5 million and commonly have maturities of one month (four weeks), three months (thirteen weeks) or six months (twenty-six weeks). T-bills are issued through a competitive bidding process at a discount from par, which means that rather than paying fixed-interest payments like conventional bonds, the appreciation of the bond provides the return to the holder.

NOTES

Chapter One

The Retirement Gamble, *PBS Frontline,* 4/23/2013,
    http://video.pbs.org/video/2365000843/

Personal Savings Rate, US Department of Commerce: Bureau
    of Economic Analysis *http://research.stlouisfed.org/fred2/*
    series/PSAVERT/

"Private-Sector Workers Participating in an Employment-
    Based Retirement Plan," Employee Benefit Research Institute.
    http://www.ebri.org/publications/benfaq/index.cfm?
    fa=retfaqt14fig2

Chapter Two

Bill Phillips, *Body for Life* (New York: Harper Collins, 1999),
    21-31.

Napoleon Hill, *Think and Grow Rich* (Radford, Virginia: Wilder
    Publications, 2007), 1.

Brad Klontz, Rick Kahler, and Ted Klontz. *Facilitating Financial Health: Tools for Financial Planners, Coaches, and Therapists* (Cincinnati, Ohio: The National Underwriter Company, 2008), 5-7.

Rhonda Byrne, *The Secret* (New York: Atria Books of Simon & Shuster, 2006), 107-111.

Karen McCall, *Financial Recovery: Developing a Healthy Relationship with Money* (Novato, California: New World Library, 2011), *www.FinancialRecovery.com.*

Kate Levinson, *Emotional Currency: A Woman's Guide to Building a Healthy Relationship with Money* (New York: Crown Publishing Group, 2011), 1.

Chapter Three

James Montier, *The Little Book of Behavioral Investing* (Hoboken: John Wiley & Sons, Ltd., 2010), 19.

Brad Barber and Terrance Odean, "Boys Will Be Boys: Gender, Overconfidence, and Common Stock Investment," *Quarterly Journal of Economics* 116, no. 1 (2001): 261-292.

Thomas Kalaris, "The Role of Control in Financial Decision Making," *Barclays Wealth Insights,* 13 (2011): 1-46.

Hugh Massie, *Financial DNA: Discovering Your Unique Financial Personality for a Quality Life* (Hoboken: John Wiley & Sons, Inc., 2006).

"How a Financial Planner Can Help You … and How to Choose the Right One," *www.Fpanet.org,* last modified September 20, 2011.

Tim Sobolewski, "How to Choose a Financial Advisor," *Financial Planning Association,* last modified March 29, 2011.

Helaine Olen, *Pound Foolish* (New York: Penguin Group, 2012), 25.

DALBAR®, Inc., "Quantitative Analysis of Investor Behavior" (Research & Communications Division, 2007), 1-37.

Paula Vasan, "Advisor Headcount to Shrink Through 2017, Cerulli Predicts," *Financial Planning,* last modified September 13, 2013.

Paul Merriman and Richard Buck, *Get Smart or Get Screwed: How To Select The Best and Get The Most From Your Financial Advisor.* Regalo LLC, 2012. Chapter 2, 17-22.

Chapter Four

"The Value of Financial Planning," Harris Interactive study commissioned by Financial Planning Association and Ameriprise, 2008.

"Financial Experience & Behaviors Among Women," *Prudential Financial,* accessed February 12, 2014.

Chapter Five

Meir Statman, "The 93.6% Question of Financial Advisors," *Journal of Investing,* Spring 2000, 16-20.

John E. Grable, Derek D. Klock, and Ruth H. Lytton, *The Case Approach to Financial Planning* (United States: The National Underwriter Company, 2013), 6.

Hugh Massie, *Financial DNA: Discovering Your Unique Financial Personality for a Quality Life* (Hoboken: John Wiley & Sons, Inc., 2006).

Bruce Worsham, *Foundations of Financial Planning: An Overview* (Bryn Mawr: The American College Press, 2009), Chapter 6.

The Legacy Companies, *Discovery Institute Programs, LegacyBoston.com.*

Mary Quist-Newins, *Women & Money Matters of Trust* (Bryn Mawr: The American College Press, 2009).

Chapter Six

"The Failure of Active Management," *Standard & Poor's Indices Versus Active Funds Scorecard,* year-end 2012. Indices used for comparison: US Large Cap—S&P 500 Index; US Mid Cap—S&P MidCap 400 Index; US Small Cap—S&P Small-Cap 600 Index; Global Funds—S&P Global 1200 Index; International—S&P 700 Index; International Small—S&P World Excluding US SmallCap Index; Emerging Markets—S&P IFCI Composite. Data for the SPIVA study is from the CRSP Survivor-Bias-Free US Mutual Fund Database.

Yesim Tokat, Nelson Wicas, and Francis Kinniry, "The Asset Allocation Debate: A Review and Reconciliation," *Journal of Financial Planning* 19, no. 10 (2006), 52-63.

Christopher Phillips and Frank Ambrosio, "The Case for Indexing," *Vanguard Investment Counseling & Research* (2009).

William Sharpe, "The Arithmetic of Active Management," *The Financial Analysts' Journal* 47, no. 1 (1991), 7-9.

Daniel Bergstresser and James Poterba. "Do After-Tax Returns Affect Mutual Fund Inflows?" *Journal of Financial Economics* 63 (2002), 381-414.

Celent, "The Self-Directed Investment Market: A Focus on Active Investors" (Celent, 2010), 1-25.

Helaine Olen, *Pound Foolish* (New York: Penguin Group, 2012), 25.

Paul A. Merriman and Richard Buck. *Get Smart or Get Screwed: How To Select the Best and Get the Most From Your Financial Advisor.* (Regalo LLC, 2012), Chapter 16, 94-98.

Chapter Seven

J.X. Xiong, R.G. Ibbotson, T.M. and P. Chen, "The Equal Importance of Asset Allocation and Active Management," *Financial Analysts' Journal,* 2010.

"Beginners' Guide to Asset Allocation, Diversification, and Rebalancing," *Securities and Exchange Commission.* Accessed February 12, 2014.

Scott West, David Saylor, and Mitch Anthony, *The Financial Professional's Storybook* (United States: Advisor Insights Press, 2003).

Harry Markowitz, "Portfolio Selection," *Journal of Finance* 7, no. 1 (1952), 77-91.

Vanguard, "Investment Risk and Financial Advice" (Vanguard, 2012), 27-28.

Chapter Eight

US Capital Market Returns, January 1, 1926 to January 1, 2014. US Small Cap Index is the CRSP 9–10 Index; US Large Cap Index is the S&P 500 Index; Long-Term Government Bonds Index is 20-year US government bonds; Treasury Bills are One-Month US Treasury bills; Inflation is the Consumer Price Index. CRSP data provided by the Center for Research in Security Prices, The S&P data are provided by Standard & Poor's Index Services Group. University of Chicago. Bonds, T-bills, and inflation data© Stocks, Bonds, Bills, and Inflation Yearbook™, Ibbotson Associates, Chicago (annually updated work by Roger G. Ibbotson and Rex A. Sinquefield).

Market, Company Size, Relative Price, Expected Profitability, "Dimensions." Dimensional Fund Advisors. *www.dfaus.com/ philosophy/dimensions.aspx.*

Patient Investing Comparing Passive, Factor, and Active, MSCI Research Insight, Foundations of Factor Investing. December 2013.

Daniel C. Goldie and Gordon S. Murray, The Investment Answer. (Dan Goldie Financial Services LLC, 2010).

"Philosophy." Dimensional Fund Advisors. *http://www.dfaus. com/philosophy/*.

Daniel C. Goldie and Gordon S. Murray, *The Investment Answer.* (Dan Goldie Financial Services LLC, 2010).

Chapter Nine

Veronica Dagher, "How to Fire Your Financial Advisor: Ways Clients Can Limit the Cost, and the Angst," *Wall Street Journal,* September 17, 2013.

Chuck Jaffe, "How to Fire Your Financial Advisor," *InvestorGuide.com,* April 5, 2013.

Susan Johnston, "How to Break Up With Your Financial Advisor: Signs that it's time to move on," *U.S. News & World Report,* March 19, 2012.

PUBLISHER'S NOTE

This publication is designed to provide accurate and authoritative information in regard to the subject matter covered. It is sold with the understanding that neither the author nor the publisher are engaged in rendering legal, accounting, or other professional services by publishing this book. If you require legal advice or other expert assistance, you should seek the services of a competent professional. The author and publisher specifically disclaim any responsibility for any liability, loss, or risk, personal or otherwise, which is incurred as a consequence, directly or indirectly, of the use and application of any of the contents of this book.

Trademarks: All terms mentioned in this book that are known to be or are suspected of being trademarks or service marks have been appropriately capitalized. Financial Literacy Press cannot attest to the accuracy of this information. Use of a term in this book should not be regarded as affecting the validity of any trademark or service mark.

Legal disclaimer: This book provides general information that is intended, but not guaranteed, to be correct and up-to-date. The information is not presented as source of tax or legal advice. You should not rely on statements or representations made within the book or by any externally referenced sources. If you need tax or legal advice upon which you intend to rely in the course of your business or legal affairs, consult a competent, independent accountant or attorney.

The contents of this book should not be taken as financial advice, or as an offer to buy or sell any securities, funds, type of fund, or financial instruments. It should not be taken as an endorsement or recommendation of any particular company or individual, and no responsibility can be taken for inaccuracies, omissions, or errors. This information presented is not to be considered investment advice. The reader should consult a registered investment advisor prior to making any investment decision.

The author does not assume any responsibility for actions or non-actions taken by people who have read this book, and no one shall be entitled to a claim for detrimental reliance based upon any information provided or expressed herein. Your use of any information provided here does not constitute any type of contractual relationship between yourself and the provider(s) of this information. The author hereby disclaims all responsibility and liability for all use of any information provided in this book.

The materials here are not to be interpreted as establishing an advisor-client relationship between the reader and the author or her firm.

Although great effort has been expended to ensure that only the most meaningful resources are referenced in these pages, the author does not endorse, guarantee, or warranty the accuracy, reliability, or thoroughness of any referenced information, product, or service. Any opinions, advice, statements, services, offers, or other information or content expressed or made available by third parties are those of the author(s) or publisher(s) alone. Reference to other sources of information does not constitute a referral, endorsement, or recommendation of any product or service. The existence of any particular reference is simply intended to imply potential interest to the reader.

Different types of investments involve varying degrees of risk. Therefore, it should not be assumed that future performance of any specific investment or investment strategy (including the investments and/or investment strategies referenced in this book) or any other investment-related or financial planning content will be profitable, equal any corresponding indicated historical performance level(s), be suitable or appropriate for your individual situation, or prove successful.

No portion of the book content should be construed as a substitute for individual investment and/or financial planning advice from the financial professional(s) of a reader's choosing, including Wealth Legacy Institute. The author, Kim Curtis, provides advisory services solely in her capacity as the President and CEO of Wealth Legacy Institute, a registered investment advisor located in Denver, Colorado. This book is not, and is not intended to serve as, a substitute for individual advice from Ms. Curtis in her capacity as the President and CEO of Wealth Legacy Institute. A copy of Wealth Legacy Institute's current written disclosure statement discussing its advisory services and fees is available upon request.

Different types of investments involve varying degrees of risk. Therefore, it should not be assumed that future performance of any specific investment or investment strategy (including the investments and/or investment strategies referenced in this book) or any other investment-related or financial planning content will be profitable, equal any corresponding indicated historical performance level(s), be suitable or appropriate for your individual situation, or prove successful.

Any referenced rankings, awards and/or recognitions by unaffiliated organizations and/or publications should not be construed by a reader as a guarantee that he/she will experience a certain level of results if Wealth Legacy Institute is engaged, or continues to be engaged, to provide investment advisory services, nor should it be construed as a current or past endorsement of Wealth Legacy Institute by any of its current or past clients.

The views expressed herein are exclusively those of the author and do not represent the views of any other person or any organization with which the author may be associated.

INDEX